# VETERANS OF THE NORTH

# VETERANS OF THE NORTH

## Francis Patey

CREATIVE PUBLISHERS

St. John's, Newfoundland and Labrador
2003

Le Conseil des Arts | The Canada Council
du Canada | for the Arts

We acknowledge the support of The Canada Council for the Arts for our publishing program.

We acknowledge the financial support of the Government of Canada through the Book Publishing Industry Development Program (BPIDP) for our publishing program.

*Cover Photo:* Battle of Bazentin Ridge 14-17, July 1916
Photo courtesy of Imperial War Museum, London, Q800

∞ Printed on acid-free paper

Published by
CREATIVE PUBLISHERS
an imprint of CREATIVE BOOK PUBLISHING
a division of Creative Printers and Publishers Limited
a Print Atlantic associated company
P.O. Box 8660, St. John's, Newfoundland and Labrador A1B 3T7

First Edition
*Typeset in 10 point Bookman*

Printed in Canada by:
PRINT ATLANTIC

National Library of Canada Cataloguing in Publication

Patey, Francis
    Veterans of the north / Francis Patey.

ISBN 1-894294-56-4

    1. Veterans--Newfoundland and Labrador--Northern Peninsula--Biography. 2. Veterans--Newfoundland and Labrador--Labrador--Biography. 3. Canada--Armed Forces--Biography. 4. Great Britain. Army. Royal Newfoundland Regiment--Biography. 5. Northern Peninsula (Nfld.)--Biography. 6. Labrador (Nfld.)--Biography. I. Title.

FC2155.P38 2003          355'.0092'2718          C2003-900319-1
F1121.8.P38 2003

Dedicated to the veterans from the
Great Northern Peninsula and Labrador
who fought in
World War I, World War II,
the Korean and the Gulf Wars.

# ACKNOWLEDGEMENTS

The author would like to thank the following for their help in making this book possible: Retired Senator Raymond Squires; Senator William Rompkey, Ottawa; Imperial War Museum, London; Royal Naval Museum, Hampshire, England; National Maritime Museum, London; National Archives of Canada, Ottawa; L.U.X. Photographic Services, Ottawa; Canadian War Museum, Ottawa; Department of Veterans Affairs, Ottawa; Department of National Defence, Ottawa; History Department, Memorial University of Newfoundland, St. John's; Mr. Lamount Parsons, Airforce Association, St. John's; Jim Shields, Naval Association of Newfoundland, St. John's; Provincial Command, Royal Canadian Legion, St. John's; Captain Pretty, Royal Newfoundland Regiment, St. John's; Royal Newfoundland Regiment, Corner Brook; Captain Joe Primm, Merchant Navy Association, St. John's; Elizabeth Russell Miller, Memorial University of Newfoundland, St. John's; Master Seaman John Bourne, 437 Squadron, 8 Wing, Trenton, Ontario; Cuff Publications, St. John's; John Bromley, British Columbia; Branch 17, Royal Canadian Legion, St. Anthony; Torngasok Culture Centre, Nain, who helped translate various English passages into Inuit; Mrs. Smith and staff of St. Anthony Library; Bebb Publishing, St. Anthony; Frank Slade, St. Anthony; Abe Gibbons, Plum Point; Manuel Barney, L'anse au Loup; Brenda Dobbin, Port Saunders; Wayne Bartlett, Quirpon; Manuel House, Bellburns; Joseph Cull, St. Anthony; and Chris McGonigle, St. Anthony.

Special thanks to the war veterans who welcomed me into their homes to talk about the book and the many people on the Great Northern Peninsula and Labrador as well as people from other areas of this province and other provinces who brought me and sent me material for this publication. Without your support, this book would not have been possible.

# TABLE OF CONTENTS

WORLD WAR I
1914-1918 . . . . . . . . . . . . . . . . . . . . . . . . . . . . . . . . 1

WORLD WAR II
1939-1945 . . . . . . . . . . . . . . . . . . . . . . . . . . . . . . 143

KOREAN WAR
1950-1953 . . . . . . . . . . . . . . . . . . . . . . . . . . . . . . 279

GULF WAR
1990-1991 . . . . . . . . . . . . . . . . . . . . . . . . . . . . . . 299

# AUTHOR'S COMMENTS

*Veterans of the North* is a book of pictures and stories of war veterans from the Great Northern Peninsula and coastal Labrador who fought in World War I, World War II, as well as the Korean and Gulf Wars. There are still many veterans from this area whose pictures do not appear in this book because of the unavailability of the material.

Some of the pictures appearing in the book are not of top quality. The reason for this is because of the original material provided. Many of the pictures are photographs of photographs. Some families who provided pictures felt uncomfortable about sending original material and opted to photograph their memoirs. This of course is understandable.

There are two groups of people who do not appear in this book but have made a tremendous contribution toward peace in our land as well as in other countries. One of these groups is the Peace Keepers, many of whom paid the supreme sacrifice of trying to keep peace in areas where there is no peace to keep. I hope that someone will produce a book honouring the lives of these veterans who have served and are serving their country with honour. Maybe it could be entitled "Peace Keepers of the North."

Another group who too contributed much to peace in the world but who do not appear in this book is the War Brides. Many of them served their countries in war times, others married our own military men while serving overseas. They left their native soil and came to a new land in Newfoundland and Labrador where they raised their families and also made a great contribution to the communities in which they lived. Some of them, all of them, contributed much in the role of volunteer workers.

I recall an incident, in July 30, 1954, when a United States Air Force plane crashed in the centre of the town of St. Anthony. Attending to the injured crew members was one such war bride by the name of Doreen Mitchelmore, undoubtedly doing something which she had been called upon to do before in war times.

So probably the next time around it would be fitting to also include these special people in our book of remembrance.

Over the past months I have had to deal with a large number of pictures of veterans so there is always a possibility that some of these pictures became mislaid and do not appear in the book. If this is so, I do apologize.

# PREFACE

Their numbers are fewer now, their bodies frail and broken, their minds scarred by the memories of war. They wear clothing like yours and mine, but underneath their clothing, many of these bodies show terrible scars, probably from bullets, others from shrapnel. Their faces are tarnished from the salt water spray.

Some are buried alongside loved ones back home in the family plot, others lie in marked and unmarked graves in foreign lands. For others who made a living on the sea, and fought on it, today that same sea provides a cover for their watery graves.

As we turn the pages of *Veterans of the North*, we ask ourselves, "Who were these young people, many of them looking more like boys than soldiers, too young to shave, or visit the pub, yet old enough to be called mama's boy?" But that is exactly who they were, some mothers' loving sons and daughters.

When the alarm sounded that the world was at war, they did not hesitate. They left their fishing boats, their farm machinery, left mothers and fathers, brothers and sisters, sweethearts and friends. They headed into unfamiliar lands, to walk on strange ground, where perhaps no man had trodden before.

This strange soil cultivated into stinky, lousy, rat-infested trenches would be, for many of them, their home for four long years and for some of them would be their final resting place. Sailing over cruel seas, which so often in the past had taken the lives of loved ones and friends, would again take some from this earth. Some flew their planes into the heavens, every so often looking down at their buddies on the decks or in the trenches. All their missions were the same. To fight for the freedom we enjoy today.

For many, the lives of these veterans go almost unnoticed. We look at them as though they are no different from anyone else, until we take the time and ask ourselves, "What really makes them a little different from the rest of us?" We pick up a book from the library, we read about their war lives, and as we do, we say to ourselves, "I didn't know that! Why didn't I know that?" Then the answer floods our mind, "Because they didn't tell us." They were the 'silent crowd.'

I know a veteran whose ship was bombed, throwing over 800 of his shipmates and himself into the ocean. Over 200 of them perished. I ask myself, "How come I didn't know that?" Once again the answer comes back to me, "Because he didn't tell me." I was told by another veteran that my father fought in a bloody battle in World War I. How come I didn't know that? Because he didn't tell me.

As we turn these pages, we will ask ourselves, "Did these young veterans really make a difference in the shaping of history?" You better believe they did. Someone penned the words referring to the 'Battle of the Somme' on that dreadful July 1st morning, "We lost because dead men could advance no farther." As we pay tribute to all those who fought in all wars, let us not forget those who risk their lives each day so others may be safe. They are our Peace Keepers serving in foreign lands where we ask the question, "Where is the peace to keep?"

As you continue on into this book, some may ask why are some veterans' pictures larger than others or why is there more written about one veteran than another. This is based on the materials provided and has nothing to do whatsoever about the caliber of the veteran. A war veteran is not judged by the size of his picture. All war veterans are equal regardless of the size of their photograph — all contributed equally to the freedom we enjoy today.

# KAUJITITSIUTIK

Kititangit ikillivallialikKut, timingit ittuguliklutik isumangit ikilet ikKaumanimmut ânniatitauKattasimanimminik. AnnugâkkaKattajut ilittut uvattulu, annugângita atâni unuttuttuit timet takutitsivut unatannisuamik, immaKâ sakkunut asigninnulu tipvuanilukuit sakkunginnut, kenangit tagiunginnait imammut sippaKillâtaulinimmut.

Ilangit iluvitausimajut sanianut nalligijangita angigganginni ilaget iluvipvinginni ilangit iluvitausimajut nalunaikkutalet ilangit nalunaikkutaKangitut nunani Kaningituni, asignit inogutitsaluisimajut imappini, unatagvigiKattadlugu, ullumiulittuk imappet nalunaikkutauvut imâni iluvigvigidlugit.

Mappitigigatta pâginânik "Unattatet Taggamiunit" apigiKattavugut "Ukua kinakkut inosuttuit ununningit angutikulojâttut sotjaugatik, jârikiluadlatut ungijagiamik, ubvalu imigapviliagunnangitut, angiluadladlutik taijaugiamik anânamminut inniasummik. Tâvatuak tâkkuasiammaget, ilangit anânaujut nalligusujut innimiik paniminilu.

Kotsudlalimmata unatannisuaKalimmat tapasimangitut Kimaidlutik oganniavimminik umianik ilangit pigutsevingita aulautinginnik ammalu sunanik suliagijammik asinginnilu, Kimaidlutik anânaminik atâtaminik, angajuminik najaminik, nalligijaminkik ilannâminillu. Ailittut ilitagingitaminut nunanut, pisugiattujut ilitannangituni nunai, immaKâ allât kinamullonet pisupviulautsimangitumut. Nunangit salumaittuit idjumut mamaittuit, piujongitut, nunivakkâlulet ititsangit, ilanginnut angiggagijauniattuk sitamani jârini, nunangit ilanginnut akunialuk inigijauniattuk aunginnak akKutingit, tamânilu ajuliKattadlutik iniginialidlugu. Imappisaukkut ingiggaKattadlutik ammalu sivunganinit tamâni inogunnaiKattadlutik nallinattuit ilannâgellu, kenaujatsaliugasuadlutik inogutitsaminik. TingiKattadlutik Kilakkut, takunnaKattadlutik alliminik unianejunik ubvalu ititsamejunik, ilonnatik tâtsumingatsainak suliatsalet unatajut uvattinik ullumi silakKijakKujigamik.

Unuttunut tâkkua inosingit Unatattet malugijauKattangilat takunnaKattajavut adjiunginginnik kinamit, kisiani

pivitsaKaligatta imminik apigidluta, sunaminkukua uvattinit adjiungilat uvattinet? Atuagammik attasisonguvugut atuagaKautimit, atuatsiniadluta unatannigisimajanginnik, tain-maimmat, uKaniadluta, "Kaujimalaungitaga tamanna!"
Summat, imminik apigivunga, Kaujimalaungitaga tamanna, kiujauniadlunga, Kaujimavunga summaumangât, "uvattinik uKautjilautsimangimata. Taikkua "Nilliasimangitut", ketâggulak uKagalâKattajut kappianattumik unatannisuangusimajumik. AtuatsilaukKunga Kaujimajaganik angutimmik, umiatsuanga Kâttitausimajuk, 800-nik ununnisanik umiattuKatimminik imminillu impaaimut misidlutik, 200-nit ununnisait imâdlutik, Imminik apiginiadlunga, summat tamanna Kaujimalaungitaga? Kiujauniadlunga taimâtsainak uKautilaungimânga tamatsumin-ga.

Ukautijaulautsimavunga unatattivinimmut atâtaviniga unatannisuamesimajuk Sivullingani, Summat tanatsuminga Kaujimalaungilanga? Ukautilaungimâtigut.

Pâginânik mappititsigatta imminik apitsuvugut, tâkkua inosuttuit unatattet asianguitisisimavân, âkKisuigasuadlutik inositsatinnik, ukpigiaKavutit taimâk pisimajut. Kinakiak uKasimajuk pitjutkKadluni "Unatannisuangusimajunik Somme-mi" taitsumanialuk July 1-mi ulâkut, "sâlagijaulaukKugut tuKungajuit angutet sivuppiagiallagun-nalaugunnaimata". IkKaumagatta ilonnainik unatannisuamesi-majunik ilonnaini unatanniujuni, puigugiaKangitavut ulugianattukoKattasimajut inosingit ullu tamât, asivut KanuikKunagit. Tâkkua Paitsijigivavut Ulugianattunit, unatan-ninejut nunani ilitannangituni, apitsuKattavugut, NanelikKâ paigijaugialik ulugianattunen?

Pâginâgit nunguvalliatillugit tâtsumani atuagammi apigijuKagajakKuk, Summat Unatannimesimajuit adjinguangit ilanginnit anginitsauvât, summat asingit allautauluasimavat Unatattinit asinginnit, tamanna allatausimajuk kamagidlugit allatausimajuit, ammalu Kanutsuatuinnak atungituk, pimmag-iuninginnik Unatattet, "Unatannisuamesinajuk kamagijaungi-tut kamagillugit anginingitigut adjinguat" Ilonnatik Unatannisuamesimajuit adijettitaujut Kanuk adjinguangit miki-jogaluappata angijogaluappatalonnet, ilonnatik unatasimajut uvattinik SikakKijakKujigamik ullumi.

# World War I

## 1914-1918

# LEST WE FORGET

Newfoundland and Labrador
World War I
Enlisted
16,922
49.7% of the
male population
15-29 years of age
150 females

CASUALTIES
1,627
9.62% of
those that enlisted

Population wise, Newfoundland and
Labrador provided more human
resources to the war effort than
any other country of the British Empire.

# ROYAL NEWFOUNDLAND REGIMENT WORLD WAR I

From the Northern Peninsula and Labrador,
Armed with the royal infield gun.
They went into the battlefield,
To fight in World War One.

Sunny August was the month,
The year it was nineteen fourteen.
They left the port of St. John's town,
For a land they had never seen.

Across the battlefields they fought,
Belgium, Germany, France and more.
To fight for King and Country,
Far from their native shore.

The bloody battle of Gallipoli,
The first battle they would see.
They were the first five hundred,
They were the Blue Puttees.

They fought the battle at Beaumont Hamel,
It was the Battle of the Somme.
Many of them would lose their lives,
On that terrible day of July one.

They fought in the Battle for Vimy Ridge,
The Battle of Ypres, likewise Combri.
They were classed as better than the best,
As recorded in the pages of history.

The Battle to save Monchy,
They paid a terrible price.
Some were wounded, some taken prisoners,
Others paid the supreme sacrifice.

The Author

# THE ROYAL NEWFOUNDLAND REGIMENT
# IN WORLD WAR I
# 1914 - 1918

The Battle of the Somme and the taking of Vimy Ridge are outstanding chapters in Canadian history. It was also the time when the Newfoundland Regiment's heroism won them a place in history as, "The most outstanding display of valour in the British Army in World War I" and the title, "Better than the Best."

Millions of men died in France and Belgium on both sides in the futile battles of the war which we have come to know as World War I. In 1914, the majority of fighting men were infantry, or foot soldiers.

When the war broke out in August 1914, the only military organization in Newfoundland was the Royal Naval Reserve, most of whom were quickly initiated into active service. Also in August, the Newfoundland Patriotic Association was formed and started recruiting for a Newfoundland infantry regiment. Within sixty days, the NPA had recruited and dispatched the first contingent, known as the 'First Five Hundred' or the 'Blue Puttees.' This title came about because there was not enough khaki cloth to supply puttees for the first 500 men, and a local clothing company supplied navy blue cloth instead. Puttees were strips of cloth wrapped around the lower leg like a bandage to keep boots and trousers dry during long marches.

On August 4, 1914, they marched to the waterfront in St. John's and boarded the transport ship S.S. *Florizel* and sailed later for Britain. Other drafts arrived a little later, and the regiment was soon at full strength with men.

On August 2, 1915, the news they had been waiting for came; they were going into action. They were entrained for Aldershot, where they boarded the HMS *Megantic* on August 20, en-route to Gallipoli, Turkey.

On September 20, 1915, the Newfoundland Regiment landed at Suvla Bay as part of the 88th Brigade's 29th Division, replacing the 1st Royal Scots who had suffered heavy casualties.

The Gallipoli Campaign was an ill-fated one. In an attempt to capture the Dardanelles, the strait which connects the Black Sea to the Mediterranean, the attempt at a naval assault by the French and British was unsuccessful. The British troops landed at Suvla Bay while the Australian and New Zealand troops landed at Anzac Cove. They were attempting to join forces and cut the Turkish Army in half but met with strong resistance. The Newfoundlanders joined in the British effort at Suvla Bay by night. The Regiment suffered its first casualty of the war when the Turkish gunners sprayed the landing beach with small shells.

The Gallipoli Peninsula was a breeding ground for dysentery and enteric fever: a misery to every man. Water was rationed to a quart a day in a four-gallon petro can. If you lit a match to the can, it would explode! Life in the trenches was monotonous, especially at night with short bursts of rifle fire from the dug-in Turkish lines. Nor was a new day much better with its accursed flies and meals of dehydrated food.

But if the heat of Gallipoli was a trial for the Newfoundlanders, worse was to come. A storm swept down, creating floods, rain and frost. The casualties on the Gallipoli Peninsula were appalling. Frostbite and trenchfoot became the order of the day. The soldiers were treated at Mudros, the allies 'Caretaker Island' near Suvla. The wounded were sent to England where they spent Christmas in London's General Hospital. They were the lucky ones.

For the Newfoundlanders and Labradorians, the worst single day was November 20. The ground was very barren and they were living in shallow trenches with no shelter. After heavy rain, the temperature dropped. It snowed heavily and got very cold. One hundred and fifty men were evacuated suffering from frostbite and exposure.

In October 1915, it was decided to withdraw from Gallipoli and the Newfoundland Regiment was designated as part of the rear guard to allow others to evacuate. The Regiment did not escape "the hell they call Suvla Bay" until the final evacuation on January 8, 1916. In all, the allies would leave behind 40,000 of their good men. The Newfoundland Regiment would receive Battle Honours for Gallipoli — the only Canadian Regiment entitled to bear "Gallipoli" on its colours.

On March 14, 1916, the Regiment landed at Marseilles, at the village of Louvencourt, near the Somme River in time for the most vicious fighting of the Great War. They were now preparing for the "Big Push," an ill-fated offensive now known as the 'Battle of the Somme.' They were mounting an offensive on all fronts hoping to drive the Germans out of France.

On July 1, 1916, the British and French launched an attack against the Germans on a sixty-mile front outside the River Somme. British casualties on that day were 19,240 killed and 38,230 wounded.

At 8:45 a.m. on July 1, 1916, the Royal Newfoundland Regiment received the order to advance. From each corner of every transverse, men came pouring out. With remarkable precision, they took up their correct positions in their sections. The rear section stood on the parapet waiting for the leading sections to gain their proper distance (forty paces). From their starting line, the Newfoundlanders and Labradorians had to cross 250 yards under enemy fire before they even reached their own front line.

At 9:15 a.m. the advance began. Steadily they moved to their own first belt of barbed wire, the first of four such belts through which they had to pass. They advanced under heavy machine gun fire and men began to drop. As officers and men of the 'A' and 'B' Companies struggled through the second and then the third belts of wire, casualties came with increasing frequency. The machine gun fire was appallingly heavy but the steadiness of the men was quite unshaken. Steadily they pushed forward with no sign of wavering through the hail of bullets. 'C' and 'D' Companies followed the lead companies at an interval of 100 yards. They too came under heavy fire and began to suffer heavy casualties.

The enemy artillery had commenced a barrage along the front belt of the barbed wire entanglement and the area over which the Royal Newfoundland Regiment was advancing. The advance continued. The Newfoundlanders were alone receiving the full force of the enemy fire. It seemed impossible that any man could survive the frightful inferno of fire that swept over "No Man's Land," yet a few defiant figures could still be seen moving down the slopes toward the enemy line. The steady walk continued as did the carnage and the number of men advancing was dwindling. A small few managed to reach the enemy barbed wire with their cutters.

From the beginning until the end, they advance took less than thirty minutes. When the roll call was complete on Sunday, July 2, 1916, only sixty-eight of them answered. When the full count of the Regiment's casualties was completed, the grim figures showed the virtual annihilation of the Battalion. The Newfoundland and Labrador losses were 14 officers and 219 other ranks were killed or died of wounds, 12 officers and 374 other ranks wounded, and 91 other ranks missing and presumed dead. No other unit suffered as heavily in proportion to the number of men engaged as did the Royal Newfoundland Regiment. Of all the places where soldiers of Newfoundland and Labrador fought, no other name means as much to our people as Beaumont Hamel.

# THE NEWFOUNDLAND MEMORIAL
# PARK, BEAUMONT HAMEL
## THE GREAT WAR 1914-1918
### John Oxenham

Tread softly here! go reverently and slow!
yea, let your soul go down upon its knees,
and, with bowed head and heart abased, strive hard to
grasp the future gain in this sore lost!
for not one foot of this dank sod but drank
its surfeit of the blood of gallant men,
Who for their faith, their hope - for life and liberty, here
made the sacrifice - here gave their lives,
and gave right willingly - for you and for me.
From this vast altar-pile the souls of men
sped up to God in the countless multitudes;
On this grim cratered ridge they gave their all,
and giving, won the peace of Heaven and immortality.
Our hearts go out to them in boundless gratitude;
if ours - then God's; for his vast charity
all sees, all knows, all comprehends - save bounds,
He had repaid their sacrifice - and we -
God help us if we fail to pay our debt.

The tattered remains of the Regiment went back to Louvencourt and gradually built up its strength. Wounded men returned to active service. Reinforcements arrived from Newfoundland and by October they were ready to have another go at the enemy. The Battle of the Somme had raged for four months. By November it had ground to a halt. On January 11, the Regiment was in action near LesBouefs where they penetrated the enemy line and captured 800 prisoners. In the spring, the fighting on the Somme resumed. The Newfoundland Regiment advanced to Marcoing Copse and the Yser Canal. They crossed the Canal and marched to Marcoing then Masnieres, where they held the line. This battle was known as the Battle of Cambrai. It was after this engagement that the Regiment received the title

"Royal." This honour was bestowed in war time only twice before - in 1665 and 1886. In 1918, the Regiment was in the front line of duty once again at Vindictive Corners near Passchendaele. The Royal Newfoundland Regiment was sent to Bailleul to help stop the enemy. On April 10, they formed a defensive line along the railway track. For the next ten days, the Regiment was in a desperate defensive battle preventing the enemy from breaking through. The cost in killed and wounded men was heavy, but the enemy was stopped. The losses in April could not be made up. On September 20, the final push started from the Ypres Salient. The Royal Newfoundland Regiment advanced from Hellfire Corner to Keiberg Ridge. It was on the 14th that a veteran from the north, 17-year-old Thomas Ricketts of Middle Arm in White Bay, was awarded the Victoria Cross for bravery, becoming the youngest soldier ever to win the British Army's highest award for valour in battle.

Casualties suffered by the Royal Newfoundland Regiment during the war were 1,193 killed, 2,314 wounded and 152 prisoners of war. Twenty-five per cent of those who volunteered never returned, and another fifty percent were wounded. Although the terrible loss at Beaumont Hamel overshadows all others, it must be remembered that this happened in one single day. There were still months and years of hard fighting under terrible conditions by our brave sons, and as Lieutenant General Sir Hunter-Weston said, "Newfoundlanders, I salute you. You are better than the best."

# THE DARKEST DAYS

In war, all days are "Dark Days." Even in victory there is a price to be paid. Yet there are three shades of dark: dark, darker and darkest. There were times in all the wars when the Northern Peninsula and Labrador, just like other areas, had their "Darkest Days," both on land, on the sea and in the air.

As Sir Winston Churchill remarked, "This was our finest hour." We in turn remarked, "These were our darkest days." Our mind reflects back to that "Darkest Day" of July 1, 1916, when many of our men died at Beaumont Hamel, in the Battle of the Somme.

The Northern Peninsula and Labrador went through another of its "Darkest Days," on April 14, 1917, when we lost four or more of our bravest soldiers. On April 13, 1918, five or more wouldn't be coming back home. And every other day during all the wars on which we lost a veteran, was another of our "Darkest Days."

In all wars in this century, numerous volunteers from the Northern Peninsula and Labrador did not make it back home. Others made it home only to die shortly after because of the torture war had inflicted upon them.

You are now about to turn the pages of our history and look into the faces of "those who were there." There are others who were there whom you will not see. As you look into their faces, remember, each one of them has a different image; the one you see and the one you don't. Thankfully you will not see the images that were recorded in history — faces showing the picture of horror and suffering, the tears of despair, most of which were brought about by seeing a dying friend or not being able to help a comrade in need.

One memory which will remain with me after doing this book is when I visited the homes of some of the veterans. They welcomed me into their homes and related to me some of the horrible stories of war. Some of these veterans even showed me the physical scars and wounds that war has placed upon them. So as you turn these pages and look at these veterans, do so slowly and always remember why their pictures are there. Also, remember those who are not.

PREPARING FOR WAR
ISSUING RIFLES TO THE
ROYAL NEWFOUNDLAND REGIMENT, WORLD WAR I

Photo courtesy Royal Newfoundland Regiment

NO SMILES FOR THE CAMERA
Veterans of the Royal
Newfoundland Regiment
Some are Veterans of the North

THE HORRORS OF WAR
LIMBLESS WORLD WAR ONE VETERANS
"I COMPLAINED I HAD NO SHOES TILL I MET A MAN WHO
HAD NO FEET."

Photo courtesy Imperial War Museum, London

A SOLDIER HELPS HIS COMRADE
CROSS THE FINISH LINE
IN THE "BATTLE OF GALLIPOLI"

Photo courtesy Imperial War Museum, London

# THE BATTLE OF THE SOMME
## BEAUMONT HAMEL JULY 1, 1916
## WE WILL REMEMBER THEM

On July 1, 1916, the British Army suffered its highest casualties of any day during World War I — 57,470 men were lost of whom 19,240 were killed.

NEWFOUNDLAND REGIMENT STRENGTH:
1,002
39 Officers
972 other ranks

CASUALTIES
233 killed
14 Officers
219 Other Ranks
386 Wounded
12 Officers
374 Other Ranks
91 were missing in action
224 were held in reserve
back line or hospital
There was a roll call of 68 after the battle.

As the men from the Newfoundland Regiment entered the trenches shortly after 9 a.m. July 1, 1916, they encountered the British trenches clogged with dead and wounded soldiers. This caused massive obstacles for the Newfoundland soldiers who could only attack after the dead and the wounded were removed. Shortly after they found themselves like, "Lambs to the Slaughter."

The Battle of the Somme continued until November 19, when the bloody onslaught slithered and ran into the mud around Frankfurt Trench. One veteran remembers:

We saw the immense and awful crater of Beaumont, 100 yards long, 20 deep and 50 across, but though it was very terrible, it is less imposing than the Borselle one. Because it is not one vast white hole but streaky red and white looking, like a butcher's shop instead of an immense white sepulchre. In our battle for the Sunken Road, we were given the signal to hurl our grenades which we grasped in our hands, the safety pins already drawn. We hurled our grenades as fast as we could pull the pins and pumped the bullets into them as fast as we could pull the triggers. As we did we heard the sounds of groans and pains which told us we were reaching our targets. Quickly we scrambled out of the Sunken Road for our front line was falling into shell holes. As we dashed through the holes, barbed wire tore our clothes and in our trench, exhausted, the enemy played a tune on our barbed wire with their bullets.

We seemed to say, "To hell with life," as the shouts of our Comrades in the front line leapt over the top to reach us. Above the din of battle the enemy shells were screaming down on us; huge black shrapnel shells burst everywhere.

Shouts of pain and calls for help could be heard all around us. As we moved forward we had to step over mortally wounded men who tried to grasp our legs as we passed. There were men grasping their wounds in search of dressing, men were cursing even as they lay dying from their terrible wounds. Others sat on the bottom of the trench shaking and shouting, not wounded but unable to bear the noise and the smell and the horrible sights.

My God what a sight; the road was blocked with dead and dying men, some talking deliriously, others asking for help and water. As I looked back over 'No Man's Land' toward the trenches, hundreds of dead lay about, and many more wounded tried to crawl back to safety. Crying for help could be heard over the sounds of rifle fire and bursting shells.

As they went over the top they found themselves in a hail of bullets. For a few moments I must have been alone for I dropped into a shell hole. I was certain that most of my comrades were killed or wounded. There was a short calm as we collected our comrades, took off the identity disks and placed their bodies together tidily.

We heard the shouts of pain and for help all around us. As we dashed madly toward the poor fellows, without fear, the shell made a fair hit, three were killed and the remainder wounded. We bandaged their wounds and took them to what we thought was a safe place; another shell dropped on us, hurling the three dead bodies over the road.

Many Newfoundlanders were killed as they went over the top and many never made it to the front line. Finally it was daylight and what a lovely morning it was. The rattle of machine gun fire broke the silence, then the wounded started coming down. By eight o'clock, the wounded were streaming down in fours and fives, one fellow helping the other. There didn't seem to be any end; there couldn't be many left.

When I found a hole in the wire, I finally got down into the 'Bloody Trench' and what a bloody fine mess it was; the dead were lying everywhere. Every officer that went over the top became a casualty.

Overhead the screaming of shells and hailing of bullets made their infernal din. Ahead it was a wall of flames, as if "The thousand furnace doors of hell have been flung open, then closed."

After the Battle of the Somme, large parties were employed to collect the dead and load the bodies onto wagons, so they might be buried in British cemeteries at Mailly-Maillet or Auchonvillers. There was also the task of burying the numerous skeletons which lay scattered. These were the remains of soldiers who took part in the unsuccessful attack on Beaumont Hamel on July 1, 1916. The flesh had been devoured from their bones by the rats, which infested the area by the thousands and made their homes in the empty trunks. Six-hundred and sixty-nine of these skeletons were buried on the front of the 152nd Brigade alone. These are some of the terrible memories from that sunny July 1 morning, which started so full of promise.

# THE JULY DRIVE, JULY 1, 1916
## ON THE SOMME
### BY AN UNKNOWN WORLD WAR I SOLDIER

'Tis nine-fifteen, too late to call a halt
The eighty-eight and seventh coming on,
All along the sight men are moving out,
"Over the Top!" There is no turning back,
The Newfoundlanders are one of four battalions
Of the twenty-ninth British Division
Of their eighty-eight Brigade of Infantry,
One hundred thousand men along the Somme
Scramble for the light, clamber up and over,
Form up shoulder to shoulder, blade to blade,
Step into No Man's Land, a cratered hell
Of mud, of blood, of corpse, of wire
Composited of steel and stench and screaming.
Thus began the Battle of the sliding Somme
As a myriad of figures moved toward the fire,
Through that flaming hail of bullets.
The Islanders are heavily saddled with equipment
That weight movement itself and burdens,
Bane of Maneuver and the tack of skill
It's sixty pounds enough for a pack horse;
There were casualties before the parapets,
Red Mars is bargain through the girths of them
And they stilled centred near their own front lines,
A speckless sky looks to their code and bearing,
Here is a day for trouting, or a westward sail,
Alas! Tis better served by putrefaction
To which will go so many of our best,
Bayonets flash back like the shimmering o seas,
Before the night will call some halt to this,
Twenty thousand of these Allied Forces
Will return credentials to their Mother Earth.
This then their posture, this their weighted tread:
"Parade Ground Formation for Assaulting Infantry"
Sons of the sea and soil your numbers scrolling

Across your Island's pages into history,
Grandly move out against impregnable positions
Before the watching disbelief and awe
Of friends and foe alike admiring recognition:
Said Siegfried Sasson behind a Maxim gun,
"The sun flashed on bayonets, tiny figures moved
And stumbled quietly to the grass
I am staring at a sunlit picture of hell."
And the kindly morning hysterical and weeping.
Still on they come; there is no turning back,
These are the stricken folding fall to earth,
That drop like leaden bulls before the maul
Sink down in windrows, flail, else still are still
Yet on they come, their discipline superb
Where Universe reverberates the strife
And chases chaos to the poles and latitudes
Where tumult tear new tearing from the torn...

GOING OVER THE TOP
BEAUMONT HAMEL, JULY 1, 1916

Photo courtesy Royal Newfoundland Regiment

## BEAUMONT HAMEL
## UNATANNISUAK SOMME-MI

"O Beaumont Hamel! Newfoundland
Adjigenik itjuliujut aggamigut
TuKugaijut aujami allakut.
Nunami inolipvigisimaljattini.
Asia tigumiajuk tuKulittunut
IsuKangitumut atanut pinnanattumut itjumut.
Timingit Kummuajut Gudemut.
Pilluat UnatattiuKativut! IgviuniKutit
Taitsumani Terra Nova ullungani!
Kuvianattuk Kallilimmat
Uvagutakilesimagitugut akiligilittinik
AkilittaugiaKavuk Piggagasuasimaninnut"

## BEAUMONT HAMEL
## BATTLE OF THE SOMME

"O Beaumont Hamel! Newfoundland
Now made twin soil by heavy hand
Of carnage on that summer morn.
The one the land where we were born.
The other holding its keep
Last resting place of those who sleep
Forever neath its sacred sod.
Whose souls have winged their flight to God.
Our gallant comrades! It was ye
Who wrote a page in history
For Terra Nova on that day!
Your glory shall ne'er pass away
May we who did not pay your price
Be worthy of your Sacrifice."

## FLANDERSIMI UNATANNISUAK

Flandersimi UnatannisuaKatillugu, piguttuit tittaugalavut
Akungani sanningajulet, nalikKatigejut.
NalunaikkutaKattisivut inittinik; ammalu Kilammi
Kupanuagatsuit, tyutsiagalajut, tingijut
Kappianattuit tusatsait Kukiutet Kukiajut atittini
TuKungalikKugut, Ulluni ikittuni
InolaukKugut, Ulluni ikittuni
InolaukKugut, siKinik puilittilugu takuKattadlugu, siKinik nipilit-
tilugu takuKattadlugu.
Nalligusudluta, nalligijaudlutalu, tamani innangalikKugut
Flanders Unatapsivuangani

KiumajotiKatigillugu akiniajuk,
Ilinnut aivugut agganit katalittunit igitsigianmut.
Ikumautik, pitsait tigumiallugu puttujumik
Ajuliguvit inosikkyut, uvattut tuKusimajuttitut
Sininiangiagut, piguttuit piguKattagaluappata

Flanders Unapvisuangani.

## IN FLANDERS FIELDS

In Flanders Fields, the poppies blow
Between the crosses, row on row.
That marks our place; and in the sky
The Larks, still bravely singing, fly
Scarce heard amid the guns below
We are the dead, short days ago
We lived, felt dawn, saw sunset flow.
Loved, and were loved, and now we lie
In Flanders Fields.
Take up your quarrel with the foe,
To you from falling hands we throw.
The torch, be yours to hold it high,
If you break faith, with us who die
We shall not sleep, though poppies grow
In Flanders Fields.

by John McCrae

THE ST. JOHN'S ROAD
"NOT ONE FOOT OF THIS DANK SOD BUT DRANK ITS
SURFEIT OF THE BLOOD OF GALLANT MEN"
THE TRENCH KNOW AS THE "ST. JOHN'S ROAD,"
BEAUMONT HAMEL

Photo courtesy, Master Seaman John Bourne

# FROM THOSE WHO WERE THERE

*"I got up from the trench; the boys were falling on either side, until there were only two of us left. He got it, he was killed. Then I got it; I got two bullets in me. I dropped, blood was coming out of me, I thought they saw me go down. I stopped the blood the best that I could. The sun was pouring down and they were shelling. I was there all day and night and Sunday came, I lived through Sunday, but when the sun went down, I gave up. I said my prayers, and seen my mom, as far as I know, but I knew she wasn't there. They picked me up — I don't know who. I don't know how I got to the hospital where they operated and took the metal out of me."*

*"We were all knocked out before we reached the German trenches. I was knocked over myself about twenty yards from the trenches with shrapnel, which struck me in the head after breaking through my steel helmet. I managed to crawl back to my own trenches for 150 yards, at 11:00 p.m."*

*"It was a magnificent display of trained and disciplined valor, and only failed because, dead men can advance no further."*

Some accounts show just how close the two sides were to each other during some of the battles.

*"Time after time the Germans crept up to the trench and drove the boys along it for forty yards. Ginger Byrne seized a bucket of bombs (hand grenades) and shouted to the boys to follow. He started along the trench, the boys following and they drove back the Germans, not the forty yards they had taken, but another sixty yards, and held the whole 100 yards. Such was the measure of battlefield success during the Great War."*

The Day After

*"It is quite lonesome here now, all my chums are gone. I suppose it will be my turn next. I don't care. I am satisfied to die for my King and country. It will be quite a shock when they hear the news about all the poor fellows being killed."*

THE CHARRED BATTLEFIELDS OF BEAUMONT HAMEL

Photo courtesy Royal Newfoundland Regiment

# BEAMONT HAMEL
## FREDRICK ANDREWS

Walk slowly here,
Be reverent and fervent,
For here upon this noble plain
The youth of our fair island
Bled in twain.
That grim July dawn,
When sallied forth twice 400 strong
Into the valley unknown,
Their charge was fine,
Their strength as nine;
In battle-dress arrayed they fought,
They bled, they died.
When shall their honours die,
Or that great bloody charge deny?
Sooner Orion burst in two,
Or the rushing water kiss the dew.
"We few"- We gallant few.
We three score six and two—
The remnant of that glorious stand.
Never! Shall we forget that band,
Or the famous charge in "No Man's Land."
Their names are written in deeds of gold
Across the island strong and bold.

"Trumpeter, what are you sounding now?...
I'm calling them home, 'Come home, come home,'
Tread lightly o'er the dead in the valley
They are lying around, face down to the ground,
And can't hear me sound the rally."

# REMEMBRANCE
## Inscription on Beaumont Hamel Plaque

Today, on the highest elevation
There stands a bronzed Newfoundland stag caribou
Defiantly facing enemy lines;
Here in Beaumont Hamel park in France
Some forty acres of undulating terrain
Commemorate that Battle of the Somme,
While bronzed plaques list eight hundred fourteen names
Of servicemen who have no know fate or grave,
These of the Regiment, the Royal Naval reserve,
Of the Merchant Navy and others.
Some of the original trench work is still there,
Left as it was when our men first saw it
Though smoothed over and grassed, softened by time,
The land lies like miniature mountains and valleys,
Along the bottom of the trenches are sandy path
Pressed by inquiring feet through the long years,
Close ranked headstones stand shoulder to shoulder
In Y Ravine and Hawthorne cemeteries:
Poplars, Newfoundland spruce, fir, dogberry and juniper
Stand about to beautify the shade,
And speak of home: Here sheep may safely graze...

Those who got farthest reached the barb wire lines
Where they were cut down in the narrow gaps
Which intelligence had thought would be much wider,
Through which 'slits' stormed shot and shell and enfilade
Through holes so poorly blown that the men must go single file,
Must wait in line as if waiting for breakfast.
Never was there such exposure so naked,
Bodies piled up to a point, where it broke the wire
Killed instantly by machine gun fire in the death traps;
Yet many of the wounded helped clear a path
For buddies pressing forward through the drift,
Their cry with that spirit "Right into it boys!"
Spoken by men who by now could speak only to the sod:
These were the Men of the Caribou, flagged red, white and blue.
Gone in the same time it took eat breakfast: Gone.

# SOLDIERS POET
## Robert G. MacDonald

'Tis little for glory you sing, O ye strong-souled and
     wonderful bards,
       Whose voices start out from the trenches and echo sublime
     around the world.

Yet far in the depths of your being there must be something
     that guards
       The fountain of pure bubbling song, and the glow of a fancy
     imperiled.

The danger has given you courage to chat as ye ne'er would
     have done
       In the old days of treacherous peace and the hum-drum of
     bald civic life;

But the life in the open has quickened your pulses and made
     your blood run,
       And kindled the joy of the singer, beat harmony out of the
     strife.

How ye sing of your life in the trenches, the glory and pain of it all,
     Of the homes and the girls from thee parted, the mother
     who
     prays for thee still;

Of the whizzing and scream of the shells, of the valor of
     thousands who fall
       Of spirits that scorn to be damped, of the strength of
     indomitable will.

We hail you, we older ones, we who at home in the Isles of the sea
     Whose hearts yearn to welcome you back, with your out-
     look, your vision, your soul –

For the day when with you we shall chant the sweet victory
     song of the free –
       When war's blood dripping clouds from the sky of our
     world shall forevermore roll.

## THE DANGER TREE

Its roots cemented in to keep it from falling, scarred by bullets and shrapnel, and poppies at its trunk, the "Danger Tree" stands proudly in the place where so many Newfoundlanders and Labradorians died some eighty six years ago during the Battle of the Somme, at Beaumont Hamel. Paying his respect to these men is Master Seaman John Bourne of Robinson's serving with the 437 Squadron, 8 Wing, Trenton, Ontario. Master Seaman Bourne, a Veteran of the Gulf War and Afghanistan, took the pictures in 2001 and donated them for use in this book.

GENERAL VIEW OF THE BATTLEFIELD,
BEAUMONT HAMEL, JULY 1, 1916

Photo courtesy Imperial War Museum, London, Q1522

THESE BRONZED PLAQUES AT BEAUMONT HAMEL LIST
THE NAMES OF EIGHT HUNDRED AND FOURTEEN
SERVICEMEN OF THE ROYAL NEWFOUNDLAND
REGIMENT, ROYAL NAVAL RESERVE, MERCHANT NAVY
AND OTHERS WHO HAVE NO KNOWN FATE OR GRAVE.

Photos courtesy of Master Seaman John Bourne

# TO THE
## NEWFOUNDLANDERS AND THE LABRADORIANS
## WHO
## STEADFAST AND TRUE
## ANSWERED THE CALL OF DUTY AND
## DIED IN THE DEFENCE OF FREEDOM
### By an Unknown World War I Soldier

Nothing is here for tear, nothing to wail or knock
The breast, no weakness, no contempt, dispraise
or blame;
Nothing but well and fair and what may quiet us
in death so noble;

These had seen movement and heard music;
Know slumber and walking; loved; gone proudly
He felt the quick stir of wonder; sat alone
Touched flowers and furs and cheeks.
All this is ended.

A man's destination is not his destiny,
Every country is home to one man
And exile to another. Where a man died bravely
At one with his destiny, that soil is his.
Let his village remember.

Now to your graces shall friends and strangers
With ruth and some envy come
Undishonoured, clear of danger
Clean of guilt, pass hence and home.

THE CARIBOU MEMORIAL
WITH ITS HEAD RAISED HIGH LIKE THE MEN WHO FOUGHT AND DIED
HERE, THE NEWFOUNDLAND CARIBOU MARKS THE SPOT AT THE
"BATTLE OF THE SOMME"

Photo courtesy of Master Seaman John Bourne

The stones mark the graves of some of the Newfoundlanders
and Labradorians who died at the Battle of the Somme,
Beaumont Hamel, July 1, 1916.

Photo courtesy Master Seaman John Bourne

# OUT OF THE LINE
## Leo Murphy

There's a wondrous eastern shelter,
Far beyond the setting sun,
Where a gallant crowd may anchor,
When their fighting days are done.
Free from "Strafing", shock and battle,
Working parties safely o'er,
Where the subs, all slumber softly,
And – there's peace forevermore.

They have left the slippery duckboards,
They have left the blinking trench,
And in parting from these loved pots,
It has meant an awful wrench.
Comes at last the place called \_\_\_\_\_
Where the billets are the best,
And the dangers of the front line,
Vanish in the days termed "REST."

| Leaton Simms | | Roland Simms |
|---|---|---|
| St. Anthony | (BROTHER) | St. Anthony |
| Royal Newfoundland | | Royal Newfoundland |
| Regiment | | Regiment |
| World War I | | World War I |
| Killed in Action | | Killed in Action |
| October 9, 1917 | | July 1, 1916 |
| Probably in the | | Battle of Somme |
| Battle of Cambari | | Beaumont Hamel |

Frederick Freda
Hopedale, Labrador
Royal Newfoundland Regiment
World War I

STRETCHER BEARERS ATTENDING THE WOUNDED IN
THE TRENCHES, BEAUMONT HAMEL, JULY 1, 1916

Photo courtesy Imperial War Museum, London, Q739

George P. Simms
St. Anthony
Royal Newfoundland Regiment
World War I
Killed in Action, July 1, 1916
at the Battle of the Somme, Beaumont Hamel

NIGHT SKY LIT BY BOMBARDMENT AT BEAUMONT
HAMEL, JULY 1, 1916

Photo courtesy Imperial War Museum, London, Q751

Samuel Mitchelmore
Green Island Brook
Royal Newfoundland
Regiment
World War I
Died of Wounds
March 3, 1917

Albert V. Coles
Savage Cove
Royal Newfoundland
Regiment
World War I
Killed in Action
September 18, 1916

Both probably killed in the 'Battle of the Somme' which
continued into the Spring of 1917.

# INSCRIPTION
## ROBERT G. MACDONALD


Because they rest in grim Gallipoli;
Because they sleep on Beaumont Hamel's plain;
Because beneath the ever-flowing main
Their bodies find a grave eternally
Till the last call; in memory of them we,
Whose land and theirs they save, that not in vain
Their lives were given, have reared this fitting fane .

For many generations yet to be.
Here shall the ancient lore of Rome and Greece,
The learning and the science and the art
Of England, Flanders, Italy and France,
Flow in a stream that plays its generous part
To fertilize the mind of youth, to advance
And foster progress in a world of peace.

Stephen Norris
Conche ?
Royal Newfoundland Regiment
World War I
Killed in Action, November 10, 1916
Probably in the Battle of Somme

575 Sgt. Archabold Ash
Red Bay, Labrador
Royal Newfoundland Regiment, World War I
Killed in Action, February 23, 1917

On January 27, 1917, Sgt. Ash went out in the front and bandaged up the wounded under very heavy shell fire. He directed the stretcher-bearers and made several trips with them. Later on he went out three more times searching the ground for more of his wounded comrades, until he was satisfied there were no more. The fire was heavy the whole time, and he showed a total disregard for danger and set a great example to the stretcher-bearers working with him. On February 23, 1917, Sgt. Ash and his Battalion moved into the firing line of Sailly-Saillesel, where the enemy bombardment was fierce and heavy. During this battle Sgt. Ash was killed, three of his comrades wounded, and one gassed.

# LETTER FROM ONE OF OUR LABRADOR BOYS
## (Trained at Pratt Institute)

My Dear Dr. Grenfell:

We are having a pretty hard time of it here in the mud. We are not long since out from the trenches and while we were in there, we had a good go at the Germans and took several prisoners. Our boys have done mighty well, although sometimes they feel somewhat fed up. They don't want to fight, but they think it's their duty to do their bit for King and Country.

I am now living in a dugout and we have a stove rigged up, to boil some water and warm some food, also to help us dry up the mud, but today it is almost impossible to live here for smoke. Our last days in the trenches we had mud and water up to our waists, but the boys keep smiling. We are still in range of shells, and sometimes even here resting, we are reminded of a shell coming through the air by its whistling sound.

I often think that the prayers that are being said for me in St. Anthony are answered, because I had some wonderful escapes. Shells and shrapnel have been flying all around me; still I have come out of it without a scratch. I have often felt like giving away with fear, while in a tight corner, but always tightened my teeth and stuck it out, and it is in that sticking that's going to win the day of the allies.

I'm with the Red Cross Department but our Red Cross is unlike the R.A.M.C. We have to go with the Regiment in the first line of trenches and there see to the stretcher-bearer, and dress the wounded under fire. We lost our doctor the other day in the support trench. He died doing his duty to our men. I would like to see peaceful St. Anthony now. It must be great to live away from the sounds of guns, alongside the peaceful sea, where everybody is at peace and happy.

Give my love to everybody and tell them that war is horrible, but I'm quite happy knowing that I'm doing my duty. Just now the sun is setting and the sky is red with the flashing of guns; when they cease everything seems very quiet. I think heaven will seem that way after the noise and crush of life. I often think of you Dear

Old Doctor, and am still trying to live the life you taught me to live. It is worthwhile and I know if we do not meet again in this life we will meet each other in the life to come. We have lost several boys from St. Anthony; George and Roland Simms, they were true soldiers and I know we shall see them again although dead in this life. I must say good-bye for now and hope to hear from you again.

Sgt. Archie Ash

NOTE: Archie Ash was killed less than four months after writing this letter to Dr. Grenfell, while attending the wounded with the stretcher-bearers.

Alphonsus Fitzpatrick
Conche
Royal Newfoundland Regiment
World War I
Died January 29, 1916

No. 1904
Pte. Fitzpatrick, N.F.L.D.
Ayr

British (Newfoundland) troops attacking at
Beaumont Hamel, July 1, 1916

Photograph courtesy Imperial War Museum, London, Q755

WOUNDED SOLDIERS CRAWLING BACK,
BEAUMONT HAMEL, JULY 1, 1916

Photo courtesy Imperial War Museum, London, Q752

# SONS OF TERRA NOVA
## FREDRICH J. JOHNSTON SMITH

O Sons of Terra Nova! Ye warriors tried and true,
A song we weave, a song we sing – a martial song for you.
For whether fortune smile or frown you'll never flee the foe
When battles rage on land and sea and the angry tempests blow.

'Twas not for worldly honour's sake you crossed the stormy sea;
The call of duty led you forth to the war for Liberty.
Your nets you gladly laid aside and drew your boats to land,
Without a thought of craven fear for Truth and Right to stand.

On the heights of red Gallipoli you met the Turkish horde –
The men who for a thousand years had gloried in the sword.
With Anzacs and with Britons there – a hero ev'ry man –
You calmly heard the word Advance! And you boldly led the van.

Constantinople's minarets 'twas not your fate to see.
But till the order came to cease you strove for victory.
The story swept around the globe, and all men understand
The dauntless will and martial skills of the men of Newfoundland.

On fields of trodden Flanders and on the fields of France
You faced the Teuton shot and shell, the Teuton sword and lance;
And generations yet unborn will gladly hear and tell
How valiantly you fought and won - and your comrades fought and
fell!

When on the decks of Britain's ships you wore the Navy's blue.
You proved your worth in work and watch, and in the battle, too,
With handymen of Mother Land you helped to man the guns
When Hood went down and Jellicoe was engaged in scourging
Huns.

Let parents teach their children to sound your praise in song.
And children bid their children to roll your fame along.
The Sons of Terra Nova Isle will never flee the foe
When battles rage on land and sea and the whistling tempest blow.

BATTLE OF BAZENTIN RIDGE 14-17 JULY, 1916

Five British (Newfoundland) and German soldiers walking wounded, injured in their arms and legs, on the way to the dressing station near Bernafay Wood, July 19, 1916.

Photo courtesy of Imperial War Museum, London, Q800

William W. Patey
St. Anthony Bight
Royal Newfoundland Regiment
World War I
Presumed dead, April 14, 1917
Probably at the Capture of Vimy Ridge, April 14, 1917

David Richards
Little Brehat
Royal Newfoundland Regiment
World War I
Presumed dead, April 14, 1917
Probably in the Battle and capture of Vimy Ridge
April 14, 1917

# AFTER BEAUMONT HAMEL
## Edwin Abel

The night the restful cloak had furled,
And wrapped in peace the slumbering world,
But 'neath its restful cloak was hurled
    The darts of inhumanity.

When morn dispelled the clouds of night,
The gentle rays of morning light
Revealed a foul and ghastlier sight
    Of hell's satanic savagery.

No sunset saw so dark a red,
Nor eyes beheld a deathlier bed
The maimed, the dying and the dead
    Lay 'round in awful agony.

Upon the cold besodden clay,
The maimed, the dead, unnumbered lay,
The pride and youth of yesterday,
    The war God's cruel indemnity.

'Tis glory, find ye such in war?
In clash of steel and thunderous roar,
In dying groans and ruddy gore
    Of dead and torn humanity.

What glory in the host of slain?
What music in the cries of pain
And dying groans? The martial strain
    That beats the step to victory.

Yet embers from their sacred pyre,
Shall set a newer hope afire,
And souls of mortal youth inspire
    To other deeds than tyranny.

Thus shall the dead, the martyred horde,
Asunder break the brandished sword,
And man acclaim his martyred Lord
    The King of Peace and Amity.

Corporal Bernard M. Carroll, M.M.
Conche
Royal Newfoundland Regiment
World War I
Killed in Action at Monchy-Le-Preux
April 14, 1917
Age twenty-four years

"On October 12, 1916, after a successful attack on German trenches, North of Guedecourt, displayed great gallantry to go and aid wounded in the open under a very heavy fire. By his action he undoubtedly saved several wounded men. The King has been pleased to award the Military Medal for bravery in the field to No. 1903 Bernard M. Carroll."

Isaac Mitchelmore
Green Island Brook
Royal Newfoundland Regiment
World War I
Killed in Action
October 10, 1916

George Mitchelmore
Green Island Brook
Royal Newfoundland Regiment
World War I
Killed in Action
April 23, 1917

Probably in the Battle of The Somme and the Capture of
Vimy Ridge

2nd Lieutenant Augustus (Gus) Alcock
Griquet
Royal Newfoundland Regiment
World War I
Killed in Action
April 14, 1917

From April 12 to 15, 1917, the Bloody Battle for Monchy raged on. During the three days, 460 Newfoundlanders were killed, including seven officers and 159 other ranks killed or died of wounds, 134 wounded and 150 taken prisoner, of which 28 died of wounds. One of the officers who gave his life in that Battle was 2nd Lt. Augustus Alcock of Griquet, who was with the 1st Battalion for only five weeks.

L/CPL. John (Johnny) Shiwak
Rigolet
Leading Sniper
Royal Newfoundland Regiment
World War I
Killed in Action, November 20, 1917

On November 20, 1917, the Royal Newfoundland Regiment became involved in the "Battle of Cambrai." The Regiment went with the 88th brigade. The brigade was accompanied by tanks, the first time that tanks were used in the war by the British. The Newfoundland Regiment advanced to Marcoing Copse and the Yser Canal. With tank support they crossed the canal and marched to Marcoing then Masnier. A single shell landed among the soldiers moving along the canal. Ten soldiers were killed and fifteen wounded. The leading sniper in the Regiment was L/Cpl. John (Johnny) Shiwak of Rigolet, Labrador. He was one of the soldiers killed in that battle. It was after this battle that the Regiment was given the title "Royal," an honour bestowed only twice in war history, in 1665 and 1885.

# JOHNNY SHIWAK

Young Johnny Shiwak mushed his huskies,
To his trap lines along the shore.
In the places that he loved so much,
On the shores of Labrador.

It was in the year of nineteen and fourteen,
The start of World War one.
Young Shiwak he did volunteer,
He was Labrador's native son.

He was the leading sniper,
This young soldier from Labrador.
Royal Newfoundland was his regiment,
This brave soldier, and then some more.

On November twenty, the year of seventeen,
Far from his little home by the sea.
This young soldier from Rigolet,
Fought in the Battle of Cambrai.

They advanced to Marcoing Copse,
And onward to Masnier.
They moved along the Yser canal,
These brave soldiers showed no fear.

A single shell into the soldiers slammed,
Killing ten and wounding fifteen more.
Soldier Shiwak lost his life that day,
The brave young sniper from Labrador.

The Author

58

Private Arthur F. Gill
Sally's Cove
Royal Newfoundland Regiment (sniper)
Killed in Action, August 10, 1917
Probably in the 3rd Battle of Ypres in the hell known as
Passchendaele

Leaton Simms
St. Anthony
Royal Newfoundland Regiment
World War I
Killed in Action, October 9, 1917
Probably in the Battle of Cambari

# BILL
## BY JACK TURNER

Bill, the Bomber, is down in the mud,
     Shot to pieces and bleeding fast,
He played his cards in the game of games,
     But he's come to the end of his stack at last;
He bet on his cards for all they were worth,
     Now his last check's up on a losing hand,
And he's cashing in at the game's grim end,
     In the shell-swept reaches of No-Man's-Land.

Bill came down from the frozen North,
     From the lonely land where the copse-lights glow,
Spurred and stung by the tales of war
     That filtered in from the land below;
Tales of torture and filthy lust,
     Tales of horror and deeds of shame,
Till he left his claim and his trapping line
     To take a hand in the greatest game.

His mukluks and parka are cached away,
     And they've dressed him up in a Khaki suit,
They've taught him to see with a soldiers eye,
     They've taught him to drill, and to march, and shoot;
He, who had shot that he might not starve,
     He, who had run with the dogs all day
Learned to shoot as a soldier shoots,
     Learned to march in a soldiers way.

They took him over across the sea,
     And set him down in a ravished land,
Where the trenches twine through the war-tilled fields,
     And the Hun is held in an iron band;
Doing his bit with his heart held high,
     Taking his chances as they came around,
And now he is lying between the lines,
     And his blood drops red on the reeking ground

He prays for the greatest gift of the gods,
  The touch of death that will end his pain,
Then sleeps steals down on his weary eyes,
  And his soul is back in the North again.

He feels the fan of the frost in his flesh
  As it stabs through the parka's fold,
And the scorch of the storm-whirl sears his cheek,
  With the touch of its biting cold;
He hears the crunch of the wind-packed snow
  As it grinds 'neath the snow-shoes 'tail,
And he knows he is back in the North again,
  At the start of another trail.

Back to the land where he fought and failed,
  And risen to fight again,
Fought and fallen, but battled on,
  In the strength of his sweat and pain;
Broken and beaten, but undismayed,
  Fighting the fight to the last,
One lone man 'gainst the lone wolf-land
  Braving the biting blast.

Daring the devils that ride the storm,
  The fiends that reeve in the snow,
Going gay to the jaws of death,
  As only the brave may go,
Hurling a taunt in the wolf-land's eyes,
  Laughing in death's dark face,
A lonely atom that takes its stand
  In the midst of infinite space.

Back in the gray old North again,
  With the flat snow stretching wide,
Back in the land of the stunted pines,
  Where the wolf and the Husky bide,
Back where the Frost King's grip is strong,
  And the winds, his courtiers, race,

Back where the men rattle the dice with fate
        And gamble for gold or a grave.

Then the flames of the past leaped through his blood,
        Like the flames of a sacred fire,
And the wail of the wind was a welcome home,
        To the land of his heart's desire,
The Huskies howled in the driving storm
        And the howl of the wolves replied,
From the shadowed thickets of a stunted pine
        That blackened the mountain side.

Then mush, you sore-footed brutes, mush on, —
        The tugging malamutes strain the trace,
And the whip's sharp snap is the crack of doom
        As it rings and echoes through the silent space;
The coarse snow shrieks 'neath the speeding sled,
        And heading into the rising gale,
Strong in the strength of his heart and hands,
        He's mushing off on his last long trail.

Bill, the Bomber, came back to the trench,
        A mud-stained tunic over the face,
By the light of the first faint flush of dawn
        They dug him a shallow resting-place;
They looked at the wounds where his life leaked out,
        And their oaths held more than a hint of prayer,
For they knew that he'd suffered the pains of hell,
        Waiting for death in the darkness there.

Then they bared his face for a last good-bye,
        'Ere they laid him down on his couch of clay,
And he seemed to sleep, as a man may sleep
        At the end of a long and weary day;
Never a mark on his face to tell
        Of the age-long hours of a night of pain,
But the smile of a man, who's the long trail past,
        Is come to the home of his heart again.

Albert Hancock
St. Anthony
Royal Newfoundland Regiment
World War I
Killed in Action, March 3, 1918
Probably in the Battle of Passchendaele and Ypres

Robert Hann
Trout River
Royal Newfoundland Regiment
World War I
Killed in Action, April 13, 1918

The 88th Brigade with the Royal Newfoundland Regiment was sent to Bailleul to help stop the enemy. On April 10, the Newfoundlanders formed a defensive line along the railway track by the Steenwerk Station. For the next ten days the Regiment was in a desperate defensive battle to prevent the Germans from breaking through. They held De Seule Crossroad and De Broeken Farm against repeated attacks and were in the front line of Croix De Poperinge near Mont Noir. The cost in killed and wounded men was heavy, but the enemy was stopped. There had been a heavy toll of killed and wounded in early fighting, and the in April could not be made up.

Charles Hann
Trout River
Royal Newfoundland Regiment
World War I

Simon Ricks
Sop's Island
Royal Newfoundland Regiment
World War I
Presumed dead, September 29, 1918
Probably in the battle from Hellfire Corner to Keiberg Ridge

Thomas Ricketts
Sop's Island
Royal Newfoundland Regiment
World War I
Killed in Action, October 14, 1918

Died only a few weeks before the war ended, November 11, 1918;
Thomas Ricketts of Sop's Island was killed on the same day that
Tommy Ricketts of Middle Arm won the Victoria Cross, presum-
ably in the same battle, the Advance from Ledgehem.

# OUR RETURNED HEROES
## JACK MURPHY

We greet you with a loving smile;
      We meet you with true hearts today,
Ye heroes of our native Isle
      Who from us spent two years away.

In all that time we have been true;
      And when from us you did depart
Our prayers were offered for you, too,
      All emanating from the heart.

We greet you, brothers, to our shores;
      We meet you with the love we shared
In fancy; for our souls with yours
      Were in the dangers which you dared.

It matters not about the creed,
      The different ways which each possess
For 'tis alone the noble deed
      Which God above does truly bless.

You fought, and that's enough to know,
      For honour, home, and liberty,
A debt we really to you owe
      For fighting for to keep us free.

We greet you with a loving smile,
      Long may the flag you fought for wave!
You're welcome to your native Isle
      "Home of the free, Land of the brave"

# SGT. THOMAS RICKETTS, VC
## THE YOUNGEST VICTORIA CROSS WINNER

Thomas Ricketts was born in White Bay and was only six months past his 15th birthday when he enlisted in the Newfoundland Regiment in September 1916. In October 1918, he was awarded the Victoria Cross, the highest military award for bravery in the British Commonwealth. He was invested with the Victoria Cross by King George V, January 19, 1919.

Sgt. Thomas Ricketts
Middle Arm, White Bay
Royal Newfoundland Regiment
World War I

Private T. Ricketts was awarded the Victoria Cross for most conspicuous bravery and devotion to duty on October 14, 1918. During the advance from Ledgehem the attack was temporarily held up by heavy hostile fire, and the platoon to which he belonged suffered severe casualties from the fire of a battery at point blank range. Private Ricketts at once volunteered to go forward with his Section Commander and a Lewis gun to attempt to outflank the battery. They advanced by short rushes while subject to severe fire from enemy machine guns. When 300 yards away, their ammunition ran out. The enemy, seeing an opportunity to get their field guns away, began to bring up their gun teams. Private Ricketts at once realized the situation. He doubled back 100 yards, procured some ammunition and dashed back to the Lewis gun, and by very accurate fire drove the enemy and their gun teams into a farm. His platoon then advanced without casualties, and captured four field guns, four machine guns and eight prisoners. A fifth field gun was subsequently intercepted by fire and captured. By his presence of mind in anticipating the enemy intention and his utter disregard for personal safety, Private Ricketts secured the further supplies of ammunition which directly resulted in these important captures and undoubtedly saved many lives.

Author Note: Although not a Veteran from the Northern Peninsula, he is still a Veteran of the North and a World Hero.

Sgt. Manuel L. Pardy
White Bear River, Sandwich Bay, Labrador
Royal Newfoundland Regiment
World War I

Sgt. Pardy, who fought in the Battle of Gallipoli and the Battle of the Somme, Beaumont Hamel, was in hospital in France recovering from wounds when the Battle for Vimy Ridge was fought. He returned to the battlefields the day after the Ridge was captured. In one of the battles his life long friend, Silas Bird of Cartwright, was severely wounded. Pardy brought his buddy from the battlefield to safety on his shoulders. Soldier Pardy was wounded four times; the last time with a bullet through his right arm. He was discharged at this time and admitted to hospital in England.

2nd Lt. Albert S. Rose, D.C.M., M.M., C de G
Flower's Cove
Battalion Runner
Royal Newfoundland Regiment
World War I

Albert Rose won the D.C.M. at the Battle of Ledgehem and won the M.M. at the Battle of Monchy-Le-Preux. He is recorded in history as one of the nine soldiers who saved Monchy, the bloody battle in which seventy-one Newfoundlanders were captured from April 12 to 15, 1917. Seven officers and 159 others ranks were killed or died of wounds, seven officers and 134 other ranks wounded, three officers and 150 men fell into the enemy hands of whom 28 died of wounds or other causes while in prison.

As a Battalion Runner, Albert Rose was assigned to deliver messages on foot from the front line to the Brigade Headquarters. Shortly before 2 o'clock when enemy snipers had become less active, and only on occasion shells were falling on Monchy, Colonel Forbes-Robertson sent his runner Albert Rose to the brigade headquarters with a report on the situation and an urgent request for reinforcements. He asked for machinery fire on Machine Gunwood, which from the movement in the area, appeared to be an enemy headquarters. In the fine camaraderie which linked the gallant handful of officers and men in the face of common danger, each man in turn grasped the hand of Private Rose before he crawled away on his perilous errand. He succeeded in delivering his message safely and then, despite orders to the contrary, he again braved enemy bullets to make his way back and rejoin his comrades on the firing line. Because of Private Rose and his comrades, Monchy was saved.

He carried his message under his tongue with orders to swallow if captured. He won the D.C.M on the night of October 4, 1917, when intense shelling scattered the ration party of which he was in charge. Rose calmly went about the task of dressing the wounded and collecting the rations which he delivered to the appropriate companies.

# HAZELEY DOWN CAMP
## by Soldiers from the Great War

There's an isolated, desolated spot I'd like to mention,
Where all you hear is "Stand at Ease", "Slope Arms",
"Quick March", "Attention",
It's miles away from anywhere, by Gad, it is a rum'un.
A chap lived there for fifty years and never saw a woman.
There are lots of little huts, all dotted here and there,
For those who have to live inside I've offered many a prayer.
Inside the hut there's RATS as big as any nanny goat,
Last night a soldier saw one trying on his overcoat.
It's sludge up to the eyebrows, you get it in your ears,
But into it you've got to go, without a sign of fear,
And when you've had a bath of sludge, you just set to a groom,
And get cleaned up for next parade, or else it's
        "Orderly Room".
Week in, week, out, from morn to night, with full Pack and
        a Rifle,
Like Jack and Jill, you climb the hills,
of course that's just a trifle;
Slope Arms, Fix Bayonets, then Present,
They fairly put you through it,
And you stagger to your hut, the Sergeant shouts: Jump to it.
With tunic, boots, and puttees off, you quickly get the habit;
You gallop up and down the hills just like a blooming rabbit;
Head backward bend, Arms upward stretch,
Heels raised, then Ranks change place,
And later on they make you put your kneecaps where
        your face is.
Now when this war is over, and we've captured Kaiser Billy
To shoot him would be merciful and absolutely silly.
Just send him down to our camp there among the
        Rats and Clay,
And I'll bet he won't be long before he droops and fades away.
        But we're not downhearted yet!

Leo Joe Fitzpatrick
D.C.M., M.M.
Conche
Royal Newfoundland
Regiment
World War I
Was awarded the D.C.M. at
Cambrai
Was awarded the M.M. at
Broembeek

Hayward Pye
Cape Charles
Royal Newfoundland
Regiment
World War I

4261 Arthur Simms
St. Anthony
Royal Newfoundland Regiment
World War I
He survived the war and returned home, but died shortly after as a
result of being gassed on the battlefields.

Noah Patey
St. Anthony
Royal Newfoundland Regiment
World War I

Absolom Chambers
Brig Bay
Royal Newfoundland Regiment
World War I

With only weeks remaining in
the war, he was taken out of the
trenches and put in hospital.
Because of the terrible ordeal
he had taken, he was no longer
able to function as a soldier.

# A TRIBUTE TO MY FATHER
## Private Noah Patey

In eighteen hundred and ninety six,
Private Noah he was born.
At Black Ducks Cove, in Belvy Bay,
Battered by winds and storm.

In summer he was a fisherman,
A trapper in the fall.
When the war broke out in fourteen,
He answered his country's call.

To old St. John's he did go,
To prove that he was the one.
To help his country in time of need,
He was a sharp shot with a gun.

The Old Sergeant looked him in the eye,
"A sniper I want you to be.
But before you are assigned my lad,
You have to take this test for me."

He gave him but bullets five,
Now go shoot at the bull my boy.
Some one hundred yards down the range,
Young Noah took the gun, and winked his eye.

He aimed the gun and squeezed it tight,
Firing, one two and three.
All three shots went in the bull,
The proof was there to see.

The Old Sergeant took the other two,
Into the can he did them throw.
He kicked young Noah in the pants,
Here is your uniform, now go!

He crawled through the trenches in Belgium,

Through France and Germany too.
The young sniper from Belvy Bay,
Showed his country what he could do.

Although back home he did return,
The battle scarred his body and soul.
Still today we talk about,
The many stories he never told.

The Author & Son

Herbert Rowbottom
Quirpon
Royal Newfoundland Regiment
World War I

Augustus Johnson
St. Anthony
Royal Newfoundland Regiment
World War I
Forestry Unit
World War II

Dudley Johnson
St. Anthony
Royal Newfoundland Regiment
World War I

Orland Pilgrim
Griquet
Royal Newfoundland Regiment
World War I

Cpl. Jacob Moores
Flower's Cove
Royal Newfoundland Regiment
World War I

Meshach Stickland
Birchy Head, Bonne Bay
Royal Newfoundland Regiment
World War I

Sgt. Leo Joseph Fitzpatrick  D.C.M., M.M., C de G
Conche
Royal Newfoundland Regiment
World War I

Sgt. Fitzpatrick was awarded the Military Medal for bravery at the Broembeek Battle. Eight weeks later he was awarded the D.C.M. (Distinguished Conduct Medal) for conspicuous gallantry and devotion to duty in the Battle of Cambrai. The citation reads as follows: "He was the first to come forward when volunteers were called for to retake part of a trench which had been lost. Leading a squad along the trench succeeded in rescuing a wounded officer who had been left behind. Though on first encountering an enemy bombing party, he withdrew for lack of grenades, he procured more and eventually drove back the hostile party, killing two of them himself."

He survived the war and returned to his beloved Conche, but died two years later in a tragic boating accident off Englee.

Joseph F. Boyd
St. Anthony
Royal Newfoundland Regiment
World War I

Sgt. Alpheus Elliott
Raleigh
Royal Newfoundland Regiment
World War I

James (Jimmy) Warford
Little Brehat
Royal Newfoundland Regiment
World War I

Herbert Simms
St. Anthony
Royal Newfoundland Regiment
World War I

Ernest Snow
Griquet
Royal Newfoundland Regiment
World War I

Solomon Slade
St. Anthony
Royal Newfoundland Regiment
World War I

George Lewis
Goose Cove
Royal Newfoundland Regiment
World War I

Ernest Pilgrim
St. Anthony Bight
Royal Newfoundland Regiment
World War I

Henry Penney
Great Brehat
Royal Newfoundland Regiment
World War I

Bickle R. Pilgrim
St. Anthony Bight
Royal Newfoundland Regiment
World War I

Back Row, Left to Right: Herbert Patey and Cpl. Reuben Patey
Front Row, Left to Right: Beattie Simms and Clem Penney
St. Anthony
Royal Newfoundland Regiment
World War I

Albert Fillier
Englee
Royal Newfoundland Regiment
World War I

John Shiwak
Rigolet
Royal Newfoundland Regiment
World War I
Killed in Action
November 20, 1917

Clem Penney
St. Anthony
Royal Newfoundland Regiment
World War I

Thomas Roberts
Bolster's Rock, Labrador
Royal Canadian Regiment
World War I

William F. Fennimore
St. Anthony
Royal Newfoundland Regiment
World War I

Herbert Patey
St. Anthony
Royal Newfoundland Regiment
World War I

Reuben Bessey
Cape Onion
Royal Newfoundland Regiment
World War I

Thomas Tucker
Cape Onion
Royal Newfoundland Regiment
World War I

# THE DINNEY BROTHERS

Roland Dinney
St. Anthony
Royal Newfoundland Regiment
World War I

George Dinney
St. Anthony
Royal Newfoundland Regiment
World War I

Elias Dinney
Little Brehat
Royal Newfoundland Regiment
World War I

Cpl. Peter Stickland
Birchy Head
Royal Newfoundland Regiment
World War I

Cpl. Reuben Patey
St. Anthony
Royal Newfoundland Regiment
World War I

Arthur Nicholas
Harbour Deep
Royal Newfoundland Regiment
World War I

Hayward Pye
Cape Charles
Royal Newfoundland Regiment
World War I

Albert Elson
St. Anthony/Cartwright
Royal Newfoundland Regiment
World War I

Donald Moore
St. Anthony
Royal Newfoundland Regiment
World War I

Walter Pye
Cape Charles
Royal Newfoundland Regiment
World War I

Daniel Biles
St. Anthony
Royal Newfoundland Regiment
World War I

Joseph Snow
Griquet
Royal Newfoundland Regiment
World War I

Sidney Pilgrim
St. Anthony Bight
Royal Newfoundland Regiment
World War I

Frank Ropson
Harbour Deep
Royal Newfoundland Regiment
World War I

William Tracey
Pinware
Royal Newfoundland Regiment
World War I

Lewis Pilgrim
St. Anthony Bight
Royal Newfoundland Regiment
World War I

David Bulger
West St. Modeste
Royal Newfoundland Regiment
World War I

Allan Pilgrim
St. Anthony Bight
Royal Newfoundland Regiment
World War I

Frederick Loder
Harbour Deep
Royal Newfoundland Regiment
World War I

CQMS Dudley Johnson
St. Anthony
Royal Newfoundland Regiment
World War I

Levi Reid
Ireland Bight
Royal Newfoundland Regiment
World War I

Arthur House
Bellburns
Royal Newfoundland Regiment
World War I

British (Newfoundland) Soldiers blinded by gas, World War I

British (Newfoundland) Soldier captured by the Germans, 1918

# TWO OLD WAR FRIENDS

| Sgt. Alpheus Elliott | Clemence (Clem) Penney |
|:---:|:---:|
| Raleigh | St. Anthony |
| Royal Newfoundland Regiment | Royal Newfoundland Regiment |
| World War I | World War I |

4676 Alfred Snook
Trap Cove, Battle Harbour
Royal Newfoundland Regiment
World War I

3049 Erastus Elliott
Cook's Harbour
Royal Newfoundland Regiment
World War I

6070 Joseph Scanlon
Bartlett's Harbour
World War I
Royal Newfoundland Regiment

3892 Edward James Green
St. Anthony
World War I
Royal Newfoundland Regiment

Henry Ward
Little Brehat
Royal Newfoundland Regiment
World War I

5633 Charles John Elgar
Great Harbour Deep
Royal Newfoundland Regiment
World War I

Royal Newfoundland Regiment, World War I
Left to Right: Donald Moore, Clem Penney, William Clark, Albert
Elson, Herbert Patey and Herbert Simms, St. Anthony

Veterans of the Royal Newfoundland Regiment, World War I
Standing: Clem Penney; seated Left to Right: unidentified and
Herbert Patey

Soldiers of the Canadian Army 40th Battalion Machine Gun
Section, World War I
Back Row 3rd from right Frank Martin, M.M., Cartwright

Private Robert James Martin
Cartwright
Royal Newfoundland Regiment
World War I

Sgt. Frank Martin, M.M.
Cartwright
Canadian Army
Machine Gun Section
World War I

MOURNING A FALLEN COMRADE
August 1917

Photo courtesy Imperial War Museum, London

# ROYAL NAVAL RESERVE
# WORLD WAR I

Like their comrades on the Battlefields,
Who fought in the mud and sand.
These young men fought on the sea,
These young men from Newfoundland.

Many of them lost their lives,
In that terrible War at sea.
But the price they paid, was not in vain,
For the freedom they won, for you and me.

Lord Keys of the Greatest Fleet,
And the greatest Navy that he ran.
Declared before the Nation,
They are the finest small boatmen in the land.

Many of them did not return,
To their Island in the Sea.
Many of them lie in foreign soil,
Others in foreign sea.

The Author

# NEWFOUNDLAND ROYAL NAVAL RESERVE
## 1902-1918

The Newfoundland Royal Naval reserve was officially formed by an agreement between the British Admiralty and the Government of Newfoundland on August 22, 1902. For two years previous to the agreement, 100 Newfoundland Fishermen and Seamen, 50 per year, had participated in training exercises aboard Royal Navy War Ships during cruises in North American waters. The intent of the local naval reserve was to prepare Newfoundland fishermen and seamen for service in the Royal Navy in the event of war or other emergencies.

The old corvette *Calypso* was sent over from England to St. John's for training purposes during the winter months when there was no fishing taking place. The reservists would come into St. John's for training on the *Calypso*. When World War I broke out, posters and notices were sent out to the different Newfoundland communities asking for the first 500 volunteers. It was felt that these men would be hard to recruit at this time due to the middle of the fishing season, but they were wrong and fishermen came forth in large numbers for service. The British admiralty was left to say, "I have no hesitation in saying, we're the flower of Newfoundland's Manhood, and the finest seamen in the British Empire." Recruiting continued until 1500 were sent overseas.

The war progressed, and German Submarine menace spread in the Western Atlantic. Thus protection of our shores was necessary and the Newfoundland-Labrador Patrol was formed.

By January 30, 1915, Newfoundland had its first Naval casualties, when the HMS *Viknor* foundered and twenty-five Newfoundlanders died in that disaster. On February 25, 1915, the HMS *Clan MacNaughton* went down carrying twenty-two Newfoundlanders to their death. There would be other Newfoundlanders and Labradorians who would perish when the armed drifter *Frons* was mined in October 1915, and the trawler *Othello* was blown up on October 31, 1915.

On December 21, 1915, more perished when the *Lady Ismay* sank while mine sweeping, as did a drifter in collision on August

5, 1916. In the fight between the *Alcantara* and the *Grief* on February 29, 1916, more Newfoundlanders perished. At the Dardanelles in May 1915, more of our naval men would die. There were more deaths at the sinking of the trawler *Bradford* and the yacht *Monsoon*, in 1915 and 1916.

In the Naval Battle of Gallipoli, 50 percent of the men who manned the mine sweepers in Turkish waters were Newfoundlanders. None of them were ordered to do dangerous duties, but did them voluntarily, like the young Newfoundland Seaman who followed his ship's commanders to the engine room while the ship was sinking. He was carrying a note to his captain which read, "Where you go, I go Sir"

Many of the Newfoundland seamen served on the mine sweeping trawlers, others served in submarine warfare. In the Battle of Jutland on May 31, 1916, much of the British Fleet was badly damaged, but the Royal Navy guns, mainly manned by Newfoundlanders, damaged the German fleet so severely that its attack ceased to be effective. There were also Newfoundlanders in the crew of the *Vindictive* which was part of a special daring action to sink the concrete-filled ship in the mouth of Ostend Harbour to bar it from enemy shipping.

In the Royal Naval Reserve, 2053 enlisted. The number killed or wounded so badly they had to be discharged amounted to 291. Missing is an accurate list of awards issued to Newfoundlanders in the Royal Navy and Royal Naval Reserve. It is known there were two Distinguished Services Crosses and three Distinguished Service Medals awarded. There is no doubt that there were more.

Through four years at sea, the Newfoundlanders earned a reputation for hardiness in rough and dangerous waters. The Admiral of the greatest fleet on the ocean at the time, bestowed an enduring compliment in calling the Newfoundlanders, "The finest small-ship seamen in the world." Also, it was the Rt. Hon. Winston Churchill who sent this message to Newfoundland, through the G.W.V.A:

> *Newfoundland has a good cause to be proud of the part she played, of the proportion of her sea going population which fought on land and of the distinguished services which they rendered. One man in four of her soldiers fell; and their memory will long be an inspiration to her sons.*

John Anley James
Forteau
Royal Naval Reserve
World War I
1914-1918

Killed in Action March 7, 1917, when his ship, the HMS Trawler
*Vivanti* went down off Hasting. He was buried in England.

| Charles Saunders | | John Saunders |
| --- | --- | --- |
| Cook's Harbour | (BROTHER) | Cook's Harbour |
| Royal Naval Reserve | | Royal Naval Reserve |
| World War I | | World War I |
| HMS *Vivid* | | Discharged due to Gassing |
| Killed in Action, | | |
| April 25, 1917 | | |

William Puddicombe
Cook's Harbour
Royal Naval Reserve, World War I
HMS *Laurentic*
Killed in Action
January 25, 1917

*As I fight for my life,*
*I long to go home.*
*To be in peace and love,*
*Instead of here all alone.*

*It takes another life,*
*The sound of a firing gun.*
*It sends shivers down my spine,*
*It's not happy and it surely is not fun.*

*Every morning I wonder,*
*If my life will last another day.*
*I have to fight no matter what,*
*No matter what I do or say.*

*For their freedom and safety I died,*
*For my family and many others.*
*I hope I will be forever remembered,*
*By mom, dad, sisters and brothers.*

*So when you see a poppy grow,*
*Don't step on it or squish it.*
*Leave it there in the wind to blow,*
*But remember, Remember me.*

Paula Normore
Lanse au Loup
1986-2001

Today we ask the question: Do the young generation of today, think about or appreciate the great contribution Veterans made to the peace they enjoy in the world today? Sure they do. On January 19, 2001, Paula Joanne Normore died tragically in a snowmobile accident. After her death, while cleaning out her school locker, they found this poem she had written. I guess while Paula was writing this poem, she was thinking about her two great-grandfathers pictured below.

John Charles Barney
Lanse Au Loup
Royal Navy, World War I
1914-1918

William H. Barney
Forteau
Royal Navy, World War I
1914-1918

Richard Dempster
Nameless Cove
Royal Naval Reserve
World War I

Stephen Moores
Flower's Cove
Royal Naval Reserve
World War I

S.S. *Corsican*
The ship on which many of the soldiers of World War I returned
home after the war

Thomas Elliott
Cook's Harbour
Royal Navy
World War I

Jesse House
Bellburns
Royal Navy
World War I

Robert Brown
Red Bay
Royal Naval Reserve
World War I

John Gibbons
HMS *Grafton*
Current Island
Royal Naval Reserve
World War I
Torpedoed June 11, 1917

Ambrose Mugford
St. Carols
Royal Naval Reserve
World War I

Emmanuel House
Bellburns
Royal Naval Reserve
World War I

Roland Manuel
Griquet
Royal Naval Reserve
World War I

Jonathan Mesher
Englee
Royal Naval Reserve
World War I

William (Billy) Patey
Noddy Bay
Royal Naval Reserve
World War I

Lawrence Hynes
Gunners Cove, Griquet
Royal Naval Reserve
World War I

Garland Bussey
St. Lunaire
Royal Naval Reserve
World War I
Born 1896; died 2001, age 105

James Payne and Enos Verge
Parson's Pond
Royal Naval Reserve
World War I

Albert Penney
Great Brehat
Royal Naval Reserve
World War I

John Smith
Raleigh
Royal Naval Reserve
World War I

Luke House
Bellburns
Royal Naval Reserve
World War I

Theophilus "T" Manuel
Griquet
Royal Naval Reserve
World War I

William Patey
Great Brehat
Royal Naval Reserve
World War I

Ted Foley
Conche
Royal Naval Reserve
World War I

Phillip (Bosun) Coates
Eddies Cove East
Royal Naval Reserve
World War I

George W. Hodge
Savage Cove
Royal Naval Reserve
World War I

Absolom Tucker
Griquet
Royal Naval Reserve
World War I

(TWIN BROTHERS)
William Allangham & John Allangham
Cook's Harbour
Royal Navy
World War I

Caleb Warren
Cook's Harbour
Royal Navy
World War I

Samuel Bussey
St. Lunaire
Royal Navy
World War I

John Pittman
Cook's Harbour
Royal Naval Reserve
World War I

Archabold Hillier
Griquet
Royal Naval Reserve
World War I

From the fishing communities of Ship Cove/Cape Onion.
Left to Right: Thomas Tucker, World War I, Royal Newfoundland
Regiment; Reuben Bessey, World War I, Royal Newfoundland
Regiment; Malcholm Beaufield, World War I, Royal Naval Reserve.

George H. Coles
Savage Cove
Royal Naval Reserve
World War I

Henry Genge
Flower's Cove
Royal Naval Reserve
World War I

Abraham White
Bartlett's Harbour
Royal Naval Reserve
World War I

James Hodge
Savage Cove
Royal Naval Reserve
World War I

Soldiers from the Straits leaving for World War I

Soldiers from the Straits leaving for World War II

Unidentified Veterans of the North believed to be from the
Bellburns, River of Ponds and Cow Head areas.

HMS *Warspite*

The ship on which many soldiers and Veterans of the North sailed
during World War I

Unidentified
Naval Veterans of the Straits

Unidentified
Naval Veterans of the Straits

Unidentified
Naval Veterans of the Straits

Unidentified
Naval Veterans of the Straits

Unidentified
Naval Veterans of the Straits

Unidentified
Naval Veterans of the Straits

Unidentified
Naval Veterans of the Straits

George Penney
Cook's Harbour
Royal Navy Reserve
World War I

Garland Payne
Parson's Pond
Royal Naval Reserve
World War I

Arthur Hill       (BROTHER)       Jacob Hill

Gunner's Cove, Griquet
Royal Naval Reserve
World War I

Minesweeper HMS *Trawler Loch Maree*

The ship on which some of the Veterans of the North served

Hedley V. Roberts
Crawley's Cove, Bonne Bay
Royal Naval Reserve
World War I

Esau Roberts
Forteau
Royal Naval Reserve
World War I

William Elliott
Raleigh
Royal Naval Reserve
World War I

Fredrick Patey
Rivers of Ponds
Royal Naval Reserve
World War I

# World War II

## 1939-1945

# LEST WE FORGET

NEWFOUNDLAND & LABRADOR
WORLD WAR II
ENLISTED
19,460
44.2% OF THE MALE
POPULATION 15-29 YEARS OF AGE

212 FEMALES FROM NEWFOUNDLAND AND
LABRADOR
JOINED THE CANADIAN FORCES

CASUALTIES
979
5.03% OF THOSE THAT ENLISTED

# ROYAL NAVY, WORLD WAR II

In nineteen and thirty nine,
These young men from near and far.
Followed in their father's footsteps,
And left to fight in another War.

The British Navy it searched for men,
The Armed Merchant Cruisers for to man.
Lord Winston Churchill, he did ask,
Where are the young fishermen from Newfoundland?

They are the best in the Grand Fleet,
We know from World War One.
They need no training, Churchill said,
Get them over, every single one.

They served on Armed Merchant Cruisers,
Likewise on mine sweepers too.
On Battle Ships and Destroyers,
And Carriers of great Magnitude.

The fought in the Battle of the Atlantic,
Also the Battle of Dunkirk.
In Africa and India too,
These sailors did their work.

On the Beaches of Normandy,
They fought with great esteem.
Even the enemy was heard to remark,
They are the best we've ever seen.

Many of them lost their lives,
In that battle on the sea.
For freedom they did gallantly fight,
Freedom for you and me.

The Author

# NEWFOUNDLANDERS AND LABRADORIANS IN THE WAR AT SEA
## THE ROYAL NAVY
## 1939-1945

The war at sea during World War II has been called the "Longest War" beginning on September 1, 1939, and ending September 2, 1945, just one day more than six years. When Winston Churchill was informed that the Navy was short of trained crews for 25 Armed Merchant Cruisers, AMC, he asked, "Where are the Newfoundlanders? They need no introduction to the sea." He then called for an immediate recruiting effort in Newfoundland. "This will save training time," he said, "These men are the hardiest and the most skillful boatmen in rough seas who exist..." Churchill was mindful of the popularity they gained in World War I, when Admiral Beatty called them, "The best small boatmen in the Grand Fleet." Admiral Keyes went a bit further declaring Newfoundlanders to be, "The finest small-ship seamen in the world."

In September 1939, the call came for 625 men with fishing experience for general service in the Royal Navy. They responded immediately and the first draft of 200 men left Newfoundland November 27, 1939. They were the first troops from the Dominion to arrive in England. Draft after draft continued, until the last draft arrived on November 9, 1941, for a total of 2889 recruits. Later 278 joined from the Forestry Unit and others from other units. Nearly 3,800 served in the Navy in the course of World War II and there were also 3,500 Merchant Navy men from Newfoundland at sea. It was the War at Sea. It involved the largest group of Newfoundlanders and Labradorians who served in World War II.

During the War, Newfoundlanders served on more than 3,000 ships in The Royal Navy – battleships, cruisers, destroyers, armed merchant cruisers, mine-sweepers, minelayers, trawlers, assault ships, landing ships, submarines, landing crafts, motor torpedo boats, patrol crafts – everything from an aircraft carrier in the Pacific to a lateen-rigged sailing ship in the Persian Gulf. Like their war heroes of World War I, Newfoundlanders in the

Royal Navy established a reputation for cool seamanship in the worst kind of conditions. They escorted the convoys in the Battle of the Atlantic, the one battle Britain could not afford to lose. They sailed with convoys to Russia, above the Arctic Circle. They were in the Mediterranean, to the beaches of North Africa, Sicily and Italy. They were a part of the greatest fleet ever assembled in the invasion of Normandy in 1944. They served in the Far East, where some of them ended up in Japanese POW camps. As in other past wars, Newfoundlanders and Labradorians in the Navy gave their lives.

The first Newfoundlanders to serve at sea were the 25 who joined the HMS *Berwick* in August 1939. The next were the drafts to the Armed Merchant Cruiser, January 1940, quickly followed by other drafts. Many Newfoundlanders were involved in the heroic measures to evacuate 338,000 troops from Dunkirk by sea. It was in the battle of Dunkirk that the first Newfoundland seaman died in World War II. Many Newfoundlanders involved in Dunkirk were involved in taking soldiers off the beach.

One of the biggest losses for Newfoundlanders was in the sinking of the SMC HMS *Forfar*. Nine sons of Newfoundland died on December 2, 1940; ten died a week later. All tolled in 1940, 21 were lost though the sinking of seven AMCs. Four Newfoundlanders died in the sinking of the HMS *Jervis Bay* on November 5, 1940. Approximately 1,000 Newfoundlanders served on Armed Merchant Cruisers (AMCs) commencing in 1939. There were Newfoundlanders on every AMC in the North Atlantic. They were referred to by some as "Admiralty-Made Coffins." Regretfully, this was true for many young Newfoundlanders.

There were a lot of mine-sweepers (many of them old converted North Sea fishing trawlers in the Royal Navy). There were generally two or three Newfoundlanders on each of these ships, and they were involved in the Battle of the Atlantic, in Russian convoys, and in minesweeping all over the world. About 600 Newfoundlanders served on the mine-sweepers in what was called the Patrol Service. About 600 Newfoundlanders also served on Landing Ship Tanks (LSTs). A large number of Newfoundlanders also served on Aircraft Carriers; on the HMS *Tracker* there were 80 Newfoundlanders, 25% of its crew. In

1940, 46 Newfoundlanders paid with their lives in the war in the Mediterranean.

The Battle of the Atlantic, much of which took place right on our doorsteps in the Strait of Bell Isle, was facing heavy losses. In two months alone two German Cruisers sank over 115,000 tons of shipping.

On May 24, 1941, the Royal Navy intercepted the Mighty German Battle Ship, *Bismarck*, near the Denmark Strait. The battle cruisers *Hood* and *Prince of Wales* engaged in the action. Within half an hour the *Hood* was blown up by a salvo which hit the magazine. Only three men survived from a crew of 1400 and sixteen Newfoundlanders died in the action.

Meanwhile on May 27, more Royal Navy ships joined the conflict including the HMS *Victorious*, HMS *Ark Royal*, HMS *Dorsetshire*, HMS *King George V,* and the HMS *Rodney.* Only 1078 German sailors survived the assault from a crew of more than 2000.

On December 19, 1941, the Destroyer HMS *Stanley* was sunk and fifteen more Newfoundlanders lost their lives. Thirty-one of the thirty-two Newfoundlanders perished when the Air Craft Carrier HMS *Avenger* was sunk in Operation Torch while returning home after taking part in the invasion of North Africa. A number of Newfoundlanders were killed during the attack on Pearl Harbour bringing the total of Newfoundlanders lost in 1941 in the Royal Navy to 93. Others were sent to Japanese Prison Camps for nearly four years.

The Battle of the Atlantic began in September 1939 and continued until 1945. More that 15,000 ships took part in that battle; 2,232 allied ships were sunk. Over 65,000 members of the Royal Navy or Allied Navies died and over 30,000 Merchant Seamen. In 1942 Newfoundland sailors took part in the ill-fated landing at Dieppe, where many Canadian soldiers were killed or taken prisoner. 1942 was a hard year for the Royal Navy; the year saw the largest toll of Newfoundlanders killed in any one year of the conflict. In January, fourteen died, from February to May, twenty-six died, in June nineteen died, in July, August and September thirteen died, in October fourteen died, in November the largest number to be lost on a single ship occurred during Operation Torch, code name for the landing for allied troops in

French North Africa. On November 14, 1942, the carrier *Avenger* was sunk and thirty-one Newfoundlanders perished in the sinking, bringing the November total to forty-four. Six more were lost in December making the final toll for 1942, 143 young Newfoundlanders.

May 1943 was recognized as the time when the Battle of the Atlantic was decided. There would still be ships sunk and more brave men would lose their lives, but the tide had clearly turned.

In the capture of Sicily, there were Newfoundlanders on all of the landing ships that took part in that great operation. The convoys to Northern Russia resulted in still more Newfoundlanders losing their lives.

There were approximately 300 Newfoundlanders enlisted in the Royal Canadian Navy. Most of them served in what was the most miserable job in the service, namely the Battle of the Atlantic on the "Triangle Run."

One group of Newfoundlanders whose wartime services and suffering details are lacking are the sailors who became prisoners of war. Some of them died trying to escape, others died in the camps. In 1943, 532 Newfoundland Navy Men died. On June 6, 1944, Newfoundlanders and Labradorians helped the Allies in their first step on the road to Victory in Europe.

\* \* \*

We have just read about some of the battles our sons and daughters took part in during World War II. Naval exercises, some survived, others perished, in the line of duty. These were Newfoundlanders and Labradorians who were part of "The Rescue Tug Service." It was their job to pick up victims of disaster. However it was not without cost. Seven of them gave their lives in this service, bringing the total of those who paid the price of victory at sea to 382.

The cost of victory was even more overwhelming. Of the 2,400 convoys that crossed the Atlantic, 2,600 ships went to the bottom, carrying with them the lives of 30,500 Merchant Seamen. In addition, 178 Naval ships went down, carrying with them 70,000 naval seamen. There were also 2,000 Americans who made the Supreme sacrifice and 2,800 civilians who found their final resting place on the bottom of the North Atlantic. In the air war over the Atlantic, 1,000 Airmen with their comrades went down in the icy Atlantic. Together the staggering loss of life in the North Atlantic in World War II was 149,000 souls.

History records what the people did who fought in the Battle of the Atlantic, but history will never record the horrible expressions on their faces as they returned from a battle with the enemy. History will never record the expression on the faces or the look in the eyes of these people who tried not to notice the absence of shipmates and tried to forget the glow from the wreckage which marked the path of sunken ships.

All this happened a long time ago when measured in years. However to those who where there, the sailors whose very marrow froze as the never ending watch ticked by, who forgot to take a breath as the depth charges split the angry sea apart, with angry blows, who turned their eyes away as their proud ship burned and perished in the darkness of the night, it was only yesterday.

> Eternal Father, strong to save.
> Whose arm, doth bind the restless wave.
> Who bid'st the mighty ocean deep.
> It's own appointed limits keep.
> O hear us when we cry to thee.
> For those in peril on the sea.

Thomas Gardner Sampson
Brig Bay
Royal Navy, World War II
Killed in Action, November 15, 1942

After taking part in Operation Torch Landings, off North Africa, November 1942, the HMS *Avenger* departed Gibraltar heading home to the Clide in the UK at 03:05 on November 15. The *Avenger* was torpedoed by the German U-Boat *U-155*. The torpedo struck the ship's bomb room which contained thirty 500 pound bombs, seventy 250 pound bombs, one hundred and twenty forty pound bombs and 100 depth charges. A red flash appeared on the starboard side of the *Avenger*, stretching the whole length of the ship, lasting two seconds then followed by a thick black smoke. The explosion blew out the centre of the ship, the bow and stern section stuck on its ends, showing its propeller, then sank in two minutes. Men were jumping through fire and sliding down the flight deck into flames. Out of a crew of 525 only twelve survived. Thirty-one of the thirty-two Newfoundlanders on board perished, including Thomas Sampson of Brig Bay. It was the heaviest British Naval loss in the North African Landing.

# THOMAS SAMPSON R.N.

From his little hometown of Brig Bay,
He left his fishing crew.
And joined the Royal Navy,
To fight in World War Two.

The HMS *Avenger* was his ship,
A carrier of size and might,
They headed for North Africa,
"Operation Torch" was their fight.

On November fifteen in forty two,
She left Gibraltar for the Clyde.
When attacked by the U-Boat one five five,
The *Avenger* would not survive.

The torpedo struck her bomb room,
Which carried three hundred bombs and more.
And as the mighty ship blew apart,
There was a hellish roar.

The explosion blew out the ship's centre,
The bow and stern stuck on its end.
Showing its huge propeller
"Oh my God, what a mess we're in."

Men were seen jumping through the flames,
And sliding into the same.
Five hundred and thirty perished that night,
Out of a total of thirty-two hundred.
Including Thomas Sampson of Brig Bay,
A Sailor so gallant and true.

The Author

152

British Navy Aircraft Carrier
HMS *Avenger*

Photograph courtesy Imperial War Museum, London F11267

William G. Fennimore
St. Anthony
Royal Navy, World War II
Killed in Action, December 19, 1941

On December 19, 1941, the convoy HG 76 was home-bound from Gilbraltar to the United Kingdom. In the convoy was the HMS *Stanley*, when it was attacked by the German U-Boat *574*. In one minute, two torpedoes slammed into the *Stanley*. The sailors on board, used to horrors of battle, described the *Stanley*'s explosion as "terrible and frightening with flames leaping a hundred feet into the air." In seconds the battleship was a wreck. Out of a crew of 164, only twenty-eight survived, including three Newfoundlanders. Sixteen Newfoundlanders lost their lives on that chilly December morning; one of them was a Veteran of the North, twenty year old William G. Fennimore of St. Anthony. Prior to his death, he survived when his ship, the HMS *Corfu*, was rammed by another ship. He also served on the secret service boats going from England to France.

HMS *Stanley*

Sunk off Gibraltar on December 19, 1941, taking with her 136
seamen including William G. Fennimore of St. Anthony.

JX247911 Herbert S. Brown
Red Bay
Royal Navy, World War II
Killed in Action
January 31, 1942

Seaman Brown was assigned to the HMS *Culver*. She was escorting Convoy S.L. 93, name for Slow Convoy, from Sierra Leone to the United Kingdom on January 31, 1942. When the convoy was on the Bay of Biscay, she encountered U-Boat *105*. A fierce battle took place with the U-boat being badly mauled and scurrying away, but not before she was able to propel a salvo of torpedoes into the *Culver*, tearing her sides apart. She burst into flames and slid beneath the waves, taking with her 126 crew members including Herbert Brown of Red Bay, Labrador. There was only one survivor.

GOVERNMENT TELEGRAPH SERVICE,

Form No. 2.

DEPARTMENT OF PUBLIC WORKS,

DOMINION OF CANADA

The following message was received by the Government for transmission, subject to the terms and conditions printed on the blank form No. 1, which terms and conditions have been agreed to by the sender.

Major J. E. Gobell, M.C., *General Superintendent*

Sent by.................... Received by.................... Time.............. Check..34 PL

No.............. Dated St. John's Nfld. Feby. 15 19 42

Received at................

To Mrs Hazel Brown

Red Bay Via Pinware

Regret to Inform You that a report has been Received from trade Commissioners for Nfld London that Your son Seaman Peter Seymour Brown Jx 247911 is Missing Presumed Killed on War Service 31st January

Sgn Director of Recruiting

A bad news message, commonly referred to as a
"Pink Message."

# RAID ON CEYLON – A TURNING POINT IN THE WAR

## JOHN A. BROMLEY, CD

On March 31, 1942, components of the Eastern Fleet in the Indian Ocean, under the command of Admiral James Somerville, were ordered to clear the ports of Addu Atoll, Colombo and Trincomalee, and proceed to a chosen area south of Ceylon where ordered to cruise in a waiting position and prepare for action. Naval Intelligence in Colombo had earlier reported that a large Japanese naval fleet had left the Andaman Island, off the coast of Burma, and was heading westward in the Bay of Bengal. However the position and timing was not clear. Our ship, HMS *Revenge*, left Trincomalee that night, accompanied by two destroyers.

On April 4, a Catalina flying-boat on extended reconnaissance, piloted by Canadian F/Lt. Leonard Birchill, spotted a large Japanese naval squadron heading west. He had time to alert the Ceylon Air Command Defences before being shot down and taken prisoner.

At 07:55 hours on Easter Sunday, April 5, about seventy-five Japanese dive bombers struck Colombo. But the Ceylon defences were ready. Twenty-three enemy aircraft were knocked out of the sky. The next morning they attacked the naval base at Trincomalee. Fifteen enemy aircraft were destroyed. Unfortunately, the aircraft-carrier *Hermes*, the cruisers *Dorsetshire* and *Cornwall*, and two destroyers on their way to join up with the main fleet, were sunk by Japanese planes. Over 700 men perished. Survivors were picked up by HMS *Enterprise* and a destroyer.

By now the situation was volatile. The Eastern Fleet, heading north-east and expecting to make contact with the enemy within hours, was suddenly ordered to change course and return to base at Addu Atoll. Admiral Somerville had received word that the Japanese fleet had turned around and was heading eastward. This was entirely unexpected. It is believed that Admiral Nagumo, who led the attack on Pearl Harbour, was caught off guard and surprised at the destruction of so many planes of his once proud air-fleet. Consequently, he decided not to engage the Eastern Fleet in battle, but instead ordered his squadrons to return to their base in the Andaman Islands.

One Bombay daily newspaper headlined: "It was the great naval sea battle that never was." But it was a singular retreat for the powerful Japanese Navy. History will record that they never again, for the duration of the war, ventured westward in the Indian Ocean or the Bay of Bengal.

JX/220907
Wilson Woodrow Diamond
Spirity Cove
Royal Navy
World War II
H.M.S. Trawler *Bengali*
Died of Wounds, December 6, 1942

Severely burned and died as a result of injury.
Buried in Yaba Cemetery, Lagos Nigeria, Plot 4, Row B, Grave 9.

Wallace Whalen
Flower's Cove
HMS *Vervain*
Royal Navy
World War II
Killed in Action
February 20, 1945

The corvette HMS *Vervain* left St. John's on February 11, 1945, for what was to be a record breaking achievement crossing the U-Boat infested North Atlantic, during the Battle of the Atlantic thirty-three times. But the little ship's luck ran out, when on February 20, just twenty miles from her destination in the UK, the little ship was torpedoed and sunk by the German U-Boat *1208*. The skipper went down with the ship as did Seaman Wallace Whalen of Flower's Cove.

Deck view of the HMS *Vervain*

Torpedoed on February 20, 1945; Wallace Whalen of Flower's Cove
died in the sinking.
Fredrick Moore of St. Anthony survived.

James Ronald Carpenter
HMS *Drake*, Royal Navy
World War II
Died while serving
April 18, 1943

Headstone of
J. R. Carpenter
Able Seaman

Edward Norman R. Smith
St. Anthony
HMS *Newmarket*, Royal Navy
World War II

Able Seaman Smith was lost at sea on April 5, 1942, when he and a shipmate volunteered to go and secure torpedoes which had become loose on the ship's deck. Both seamen were swept overboard and lost at sea. A tombstone bearing Seaman Smith's name marks an empty grave in the churchyard at Fishing Point, St. Anthony, overlooking the sea — a place where he visited many times as a boy.

HMS *Newmarket*

From which Seaman Edward Smith lost his life

181221 Robert Simms
St. Anthony
Killed in Action
August 26, 1940

181687 Joseph Richards
St. Carols
Killed in Action
August 16, 1940

On June 16, 1940, they survived the sinking of their ship, the Armed Merchant Cruiser, HMS *Andania*, off the coast of Iceland by a German U-Boat, but the cards were stacked against the two Veterans of the North. They were both killed in an air raid at Plymouth when the R.N. Barracks at HMS *Drake* was bombed.

JX216657 Charles N. Hancock
St. Anthony
Royal Navy, World War II
Killed in Action
May 7, 1944

JX246717 Wilfred J. Noble
Big Brehat
Royal Navy, World War II
Killed in Action
May 7, 1944

Charles Hancock and Wilfred Noble were heading home on a well deserved leave from the Royal Navy. They hitched a passage on the HMCS Canadian Destroyer *Valleyfield*, which was heading for Newfoundland. As the ship migrated through ice-bergy waters on that May 7 night, 1944, the destroyer was attacked by the German U-boat *548*. As the torpedo ripped into the port side, a tremendous explosion occurred as part of the ship flew skyward and a mast of the battleship severed itself from their ship. There was a roar of escaping steam as the ship settled into the water.

Choking with thick oil which filled their eyes, mouth and noses, the seamen huddled together in the freezing water and watched as the ship disappeared beneath the waves. A freezing silence fell over the dark sea as 115 brave men lost their lives that night, including two Veterans of the North; Charles Hancock and Wilfred Noble. The U-boat which sank the *Valleyfield* was sunk on April 20, 1945, by four United States Destroyer escort ships.

HMCS *Valleyfield*

Sank on May 7, 1944. Charles Hancock and Wilfred Noble perished along with 113 other men.

Photograph courtesy of National Archives of Canada, PA-178722

Sub. Lieut. Fredrick Moore
St. Anthony
HMS *Vervain*
Royal Navy
World War II

One of the officers who survived the sinking of the HMS *Vervain* when Seaman Wallace Whalen of Flower's Cove died was Sub. Lieut. Moores, who was mentioned in dispatches which read:

"FOR BRAVERY, GOOD SEAMANSHIP AND INSPIRING DEVO-
TIONS TO DUTY IN DAMAGE CONTROL, UNDER EXACTING
CONDITIONS WHILE SERVING ON HMS *VERVAIN*."

It was classed as one of the most dangerous missions of the naval war, Mine Sweeping, or patrol service as they were called. Many Newfoundlanders and Labradorians served on these Mine Sweepers, which in most parts were old converted British Fishing Trawlers. When the Royal Navy was short of men to crew these Mines Sweepers, Churchill asked, "Where are those young Newfoundland fishermen? Bring them over, they don't need any training."

Reuben Patey (SHIPMATE) Absolom Colbourne
Little Brehat St. Anthony
Royal Navy Royal Navy
World War II World War II

Mine Sweeper *BYMS 807*

# SPLICE THE MAIN-BRACE
John Bromley, CD

I was a twenty-one-year old Able Seaman on HMS *Revenge*, a 32,000 ton battleship, soon to experience a rare but time-honoured ritual of the Royal Navy – downing a double tot (3 ounces) of neat, navy rum.

We were in the Indian Ocean, heading for Singapore as part of the Eastern Fleet. It's early morning and suddenly the ship's intercom came to life: "Attention, all hands! This is the Captain speaking. Word has just been received from London that the Japanese Imperial Navy has carried out a devastating attack on Pearl Harbour, resulting in extensive damage to naval ships and shore establishments. President Roosevelt has declared war on Japan and the Axis Powers. We will carry on to our destination. God save the King!...And Splice the Main-Brace." The date: December 7, 1941.

"Splice the main-brace" is a Royal prerogative, and is only granted on very special occasions; so we wondered who in London gave permission to "celebrate." For certain there would be no rejoicing over the sinking of half the American fleet, but we were sure as hell glad that the Yanks were finally in the war.

The directive came from King George VI himself, the *Revenge* being the only ship in the area to be so honoured. We knew that His Majesty harboured a nostalgic bent for the *Revenge*, and often inquired as to her whereabouts. Once while on the Halifax-Londonderry run, after a particularly rough crossing, having lost three ships to German "wolf-packs," the King paid us a visit in Liverpool. He was accompanied by Prime Minister Churchill, who lumbered up the gangway behind the King, chewing on that infernal cigar and growling away to himself, obviously displeased at being dragged out in the cold to inspect a bunch of half-frozen sailors. But the King had his reasons. As Prince Albert, Duke of York, he served on the *Revenge* as a 19-year old midshipman. At the time, the First World War was raging, and the Throne of England was not uppermost in his mind.

The *Revenge* was his first ship. Why shouldn't he wax sentimental over the old battlewagon? For that also is a King's prerogative.

HMS *Revenge*

The ship on which several Veterans of the North sailed

Churchill Mitchelmore
St. Anthony
Royal Navy, Mine Sweeping
World War II
Survived a sinking

Bede Stone
Henley Harbour
Royal Navy
World War II

Donald Hillier
Griquet
Royal Navy
World War II

(BROTHER)

Francis Hillier
Griquet
Royal Navy
World War II

Royal Navy, World War II

Left to Right: Wallace Whalen, Flower's Cove, John Dumaresque ?
Forteau, and Gilbert Noseworthy, Green Island Brook

Lt. Cdr. C.L. (Lea) Gillard
Englee
Protestant Chaplain Afloat, Royal Canadian Navy
World War II
H.M.C.S. *Prince David*

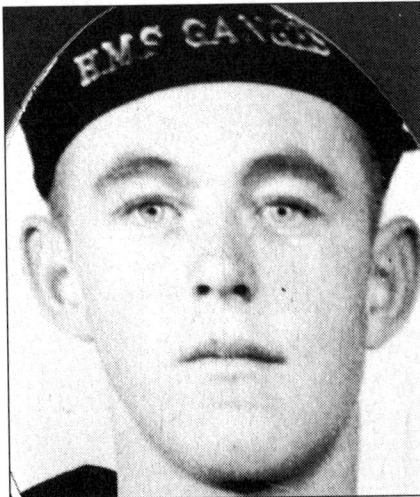

Francis (Frank) Simms
St. Anthony
Royal Navy, World War II
mentioned in dispatches

HMS Aircraft Carrier *Ark Royal*

Some of our veterans served aboard this ship

Left to Right: Unidentified, Unidentified and Henry Winters
St. Anthony, Royal Navy, World War II

Left to Right: Absolom
Chambers, George Chambers
and Henry Galliott
Royal Navy
World War II

Rene Canning
Roddickton
Royal Navy
World War II

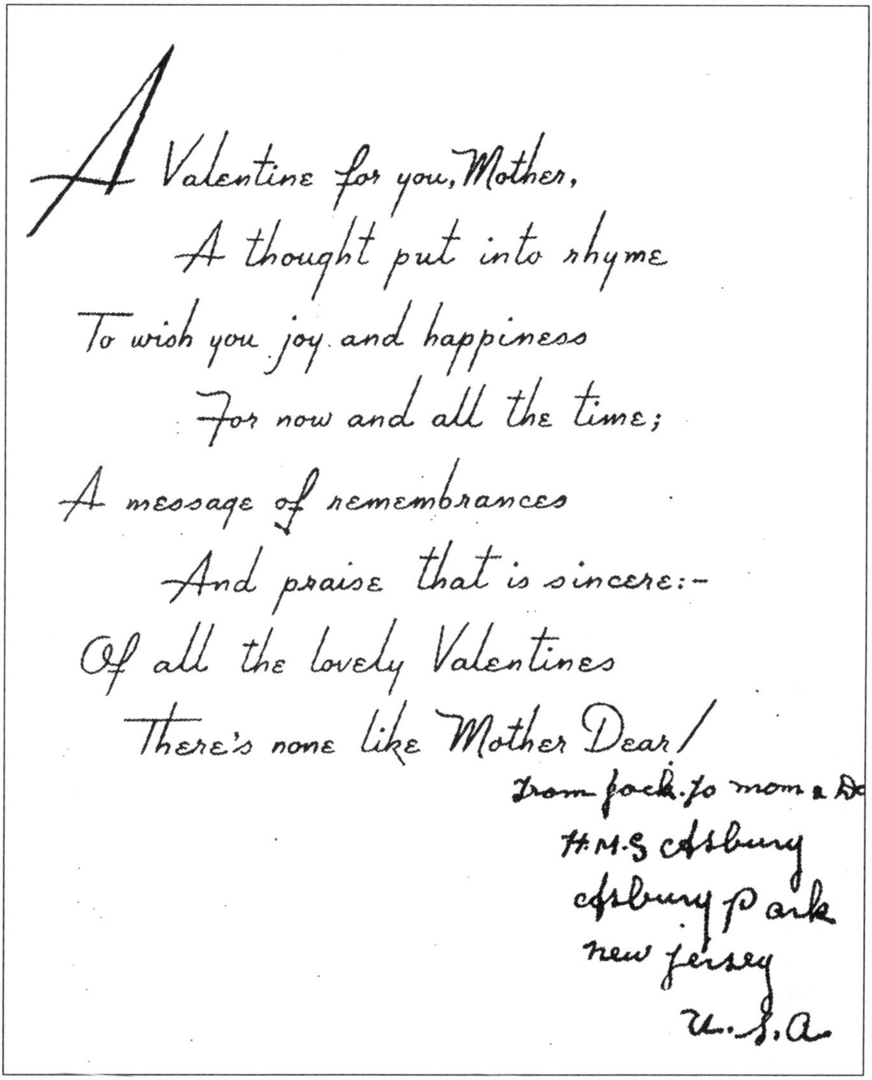

A Valentine for you, Mother,
   A thought put into rhyme
To wish you joy and happiness
   For now and all the time;
A message of remembrances
   And praise that is sincere:-
Of all the lovely Valentines
   There's none like Mother Dear!

from Jock. to mom & Dr
H.M.S Asbury
Asbury Park
new Jersey
U.S.a

This Valentine was sent by Seaman John Luther, Royal Navy,
World War II, to his mother in Battle Harbour, Labrador.

Walter Shears
Rocky Harbour
Royal Navy
World War II

Harry Bradley
Indian Cove
Royal Navy
World War II

Roland Roberts
Woody Point
Royal Navy
World War II

Edgar Decker
Ship Cove/Cape Onion
Royal Navy
World War II

German Battleship *Bismark* engaging HMS *Hood*

Photograph courtesy of Imperial War Museum, London, 15931

Patrick Fogarty
Winterhouse Brook
Forestry
World War II

(BROTHER)

Joseph Fogarty
Winterhouse Brook
Royal Navy
World War II

John Luther
Battle Harbour
Royal Navy
World War II

Haylock Decker
Cape Onion
Royal Navy
World War II

Levi F. Reid
Ireland Bight          (BUDDY)
Royal Navy
World War II

Cornelious Biggin
Daniel's Harbour
Royal Navy
World War II

Daniel B. Power
Conche
Royal Navy
World War II

Henry W. Galliott
Eddies Cove West
Royal Navy
World War II

(TWIN BROTHER)

| Edgar Hedderson | Heber Hedderson |
|---|---|
| Noddy Bay | Noddy Bay |
| Royal Navy | British Army |
| World War II | World War II |

| Roland (Mick) Ollerhead | Cornelious Guinchard |
|---|---|
| Main Brook | Daniel's Harbour |
| Royal Navy/Forestry | Royal Navy |
| World War II | World War II |

Smoke rising from the wreck of the HMS *Hood*

Photograph courtesy of Imperial War Museum, London, HU384

Lt. JX246709
Fremontia Augustus Cull
Great Brehat
Royal Navy
World War II

A war lifetime on Mine Sweepers. His awards, AIX-Anti Submarine and Minesweeping badge, Silver Badge, March 12, 1945. Three War Services Chevrons, April 11, 1944, September 3, 1944, WSI (3) and October 6, 1944, WSE (4).

He was discharged May 19, 1945, for health reasons and suffered the effects of the war for his lifetime.

Lt. JX265194
Leonard Biggin, DSM
Daniel's Harbour
Royal Navy
World War II

HMT *Wateyly*: January 2, 1943, birthday honours list 1943 for gallantry and outstanding service in the face of the enemy and for zeal. Patience and cheerfulness in the dangerous waters and for setting an example of the whole hearted devotion to duty without which the high tradition of the Royal Navy could not have been upheld.

John Willette
Winterhouse Brook
Royal Navy
World War II

Stanley Kennedy
Winterhouse Brook
Royal Navy
World War II

HMS *Liverpool*

The ship of Henry Galliott and other Veterans of the North

Leading Seaman, Sgt. John A Bromley
Grey Islands/N.E. Crouse
Royal Navy, World War II, Korean War 1950-53
Peace Keeping, Germany, Cyprus and Egypt

Joined Battleship HMS *Revenge* in February 1941. Was involved in convoy duty in the North Atlantic in 1941 which was a struggle for survival. On the Halifax-Londonderry run, in combat with the German U-boats known as the "Wolf Pack". In November joined the Eastern Fleet, was in the Indian Ocean during the Attack on Pearl Harbour. In 1942 was in the Indian Ocean, Bay of Bengal, Gulf of Aden and the Arabian Sea. Served on HMS *Victory*, and HMS *Excellent*, completing a gunnery and assault course. Then assigned to Anti-Aircraft defence site on harbour docks in Portsmouth. Served on HMS *Shropshire*, HMS *Duckworth*, HMS *Eastway*, HMS *Avalon*, and HMCS *Lockport*, a Canadian Minesweeper. Joined the Canadian Army in 1950, served in the Korean War with the Canadian Movement Control Group, stationed at Tokchong, transferred to Panmunjom near the 38th Parallel. He also served at Kimpo Airport. His final posting was in the far East at Henada Airport Tokyo, Japan. Also served in Peace Keeping duties in Germany, Cyprus and Egypt.

# HERALDRY — CRESTS, INSIGNIA, AND MOTTOES
## John A. Bromley, CD

Veterans of the Armed Forces will recall the insignia and mottoes inscribed on their belt buckets and hat badges. I can remember that motto on my arm belt buckle: "Rien sans labeur" (Nothing without labour).

Heraldry, and its attributive symbols, began in prehistoric times. I am always fascinated, however, with English, Irish and French history as it relates to the creation and awarding of crests, coats-of-arms, shields, badges and banners, together with their inscribed mottoes. The awards were generally associated with battle honours and chivalry.

Traditionally, the mottoes were in French or Latin, the origins of which many are untraceable, lost in the mist of time. One of the most honourable and ancient of Orders and its ascribed motto, originated in the form of a rebuke during the reign of Edward III (1312-1377) who managed to keep his crown – and his head – for fifty turbulent years.

Edward III was a warrior king. He was a popular but autocratic monarch, who between wars brought a measure of stability to his fractious realm. He was also the father of the Black Prince; who wasn't black. The Prince was a 6'6" blond, blue-eyed giant of a man, who burnished his battle armour to a shiny black luster. Like his famous father, he scared the daylights out of his opponents. He died of untreated combat wounds at age 46 and is buried in Canterbury Cathedral. The inscription on his tomb reads:"Houmout – Ich Bien" (High courage – I serve.)

One night at a gala ball being held in the Royal Court, the King was dancing with a lady of great charm and beauty, when suddenly her garter snapped and fell to the floor. The music stopped, and there was a hush as the revelers stared at the embarrassed lady and dainty feminine raiment at her feet. Edward, composed but obviously annoyed, cast a regal eye on his courtiers and admonished: "Honi soit qui y pense" (Evil to him who evil thinks).

Thus the inception of the most conveyed and prestigious laurel in the annals of Royal Heraldry: The Order of the Garter.

Willis (Dick) Pardy   (BROTHER)   Elmer C. Pardy
St. Anthony                             St. Anthony
Royal Navy                          Royal Navy
World War II                     World War II

Patrick O'Neill                  Petty Officer
Conche                        Thomas Dunphy
Royal Navy                     Royal Navy
World War II                 World War II

Leonard Elliott
Cook's Harbour
Royal Navy
World War II

Abil Pynn
Raleigh
Royal Navy
World War II

HMS *Rodney* firing on German Battleship *Bismark*

Photograph courtesy of Imperial War Museum, London, 15931

Anthony Reardon
Goose Cove
Royal Navy
World War II

James Reardon
Goose Cove
Royal Navy
World War II

Gordon House
Bellburns
Royal Navy/Forestry
World War II

Stanley Patey
St. Anthony
Royal Navy
World War II

HMS *Rodney*, the final of the five HMS ships to pound the pride of the German Navy, the *Bismark*. The *Bismark* was merciless until it went to the bottom in 2500 fathoms of water in the Denmark Strait, May 27, 1941. The other HMS ships were the HMS *Ark Royal, King George V, Northfolk,* and *Dorsetshire*.

Veterans of the North Seaman Abraham (Abe) Brown of Wild Bight was a crew member of the *Rodney* and was involved in the sinking.

Herbert Andrews
St. Anthony
Royal Navy
World War II

Roland Tucker
Cape Onion
Royal Navy
World War II

Reuben Simms
St. Anthony
Royal Navy
World War II

Herbert Sheppard
Brig Bay
Royal Navy
World War II

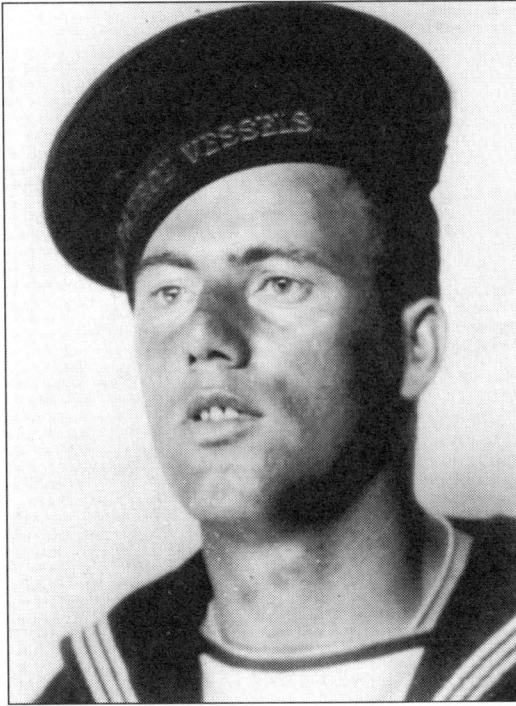

Brendon B. Dobbin
Port Saunders
Forestry/Royal Navy
World War II

Assignment — Mine Sweeping in the English Channel. During the Battle of Normandy he helped evacuate the wounded from the beaches and transported them to hospitals in England. He remembered when, "there were times when you couldn't see up through the sky for planes. By this time I was hardened to battle, having survived two torpedo sinkings, and in the water for hours waiting to be rescued."

Mr. Dobbin was awarded the 1939-1945 Star, Battle of Britain Atlantic Star, Air Crew Europe Defence Medal, Silver Laurel Leaves, King's Commendation for Bravery, War Medal 1939-45 Oak Leaf, and Newfoundland Volunteer Service Medal, 1939-1945.

Wesley Biles
St. Anthony
Royal Navy
World War II

William H. Bessey
Cape Onion
Royal Navy
World War II

Horace Beaufield
Raleigh
Royal Navy
World War II

Andrew Gould
Bear Cove
Royal Navy
World War II

Douglas Brett
Sop's Arm
Royal Navy
World War II

Edward Whalen
Shoal Cove
Royal Navy
World War II

Robert Solomon Perry
Fox Harbour, Labrador
Royal Navy
World War II

Alexander (Alex) Simms
St. Anthony
Royal Navy
World War II

Bernard Casey
Conche
Royal Navy
World War II

Leo Troy
Goose Cove
Royal Navy
World War II

Both Seamen Troy and Casey were assigned to a L.S.T. (Landing Ship Tank) in the Invasion of Sicily, when their landing tank was sunk. Both seamen spent many hours in the water before being rescued during which time Seaman Troy credited Seaman Casey for saving his life. Suffering from shock and hypothermia, Seaman Troy was taken to Bermuda Hospital where he spent three months. When he was well enough to walk, he was transferred to the hospital in St. John's where he spent the winter. In July 1944, he was given a discharge from the Navy for medical reasons. Years after the war ended he said, "I was never the same since."

Freeman Green
St. Anthony
Royal Navy
World War II

William Whalen
Conche
Royal Navy
World War II

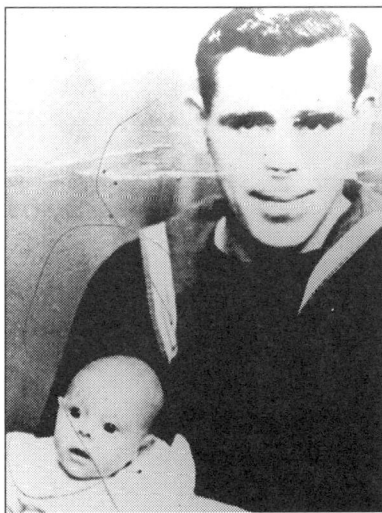

Lionel Noseworthy & War Baby
Green Island Brook
Royal Navy
World War II

Abraham Brown
Wild Bight
Royal Navy, World War II
Helped to sink the *Bismark*

Harvey Penney
Cook's Harbour
Royal Navy
World War II

Charles Tucker
Cave Onion/Ship Cove
Royal Navy
World War II

## BROTHERS CONTRIBUTION TO WORLD PEACE

| Absalom Chambers | Ronald Chambers | George Chambers |
| --- | --- | --- |
| Barr'd Harbour | Barr'd Harbour | Barr'd Harbour |
| Royal Navy | Forestry | Royal Navy |
| World War II | World War II | World War II |

Absalom Chambers in the barrel of his ship's cannon

Herbert Andrews
St. Anthony
Royal Navy
World War II

Archabold Andrews
St. Anthony
Forestry
World War II

Anthony Reardon
Goose Cove
Royal Navy
World War II

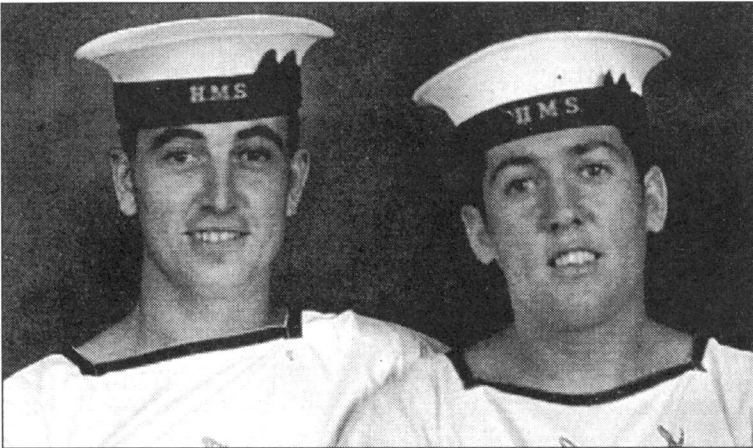

Douglas Brett
Sop's Arm
Royal Navy
World War II

Gordon Osmond
Sop's Arm
Royal Navy
World War II

Everton Strangemore
St. Anthony
Royal Navy
World War II

The HMS *Fiji* was part of a force of cruisers and destroyers charged with the duty of preventing Italian convoys running from Greece to Crete with reinforcements and supplies. On the morning of May 22, 1941, a convoy was reported south of the Island of Milos. In the afternoon the HMS *Grayhound* was sunk. The *Fiji* and the HMS *Gloucester* were assigned to pick up the survivors from the *Grayhound* when the *Gloucester* too was sunk. This left the *Fiji* to fend for itself against an overwhelming force of German planes. After shooting down a number of them, the ship was hit and damaged. Crippled to a reduced speed, the *Fiji* was attacked a second time and sunk off the Island of Antikithera just before nightfall. The loss of life was 224 men and the 334 survivors were picked up by the HMS *Kandahar* and *Kingston*, including Everton Strangemore of St. Anthony.

HMS *Fiji*

Sunk May 22, 1941

Presentation of a picture of Her Majesty Queen Elizabeth II to the
Royal Canadian Legion Branch 55 Plum Point.
Left to Right: Senator Jack Marshall, Henry Tucker and Abe
Gibbons

Veterans of the North on parade, Branch 55 Plum Point. Flag
Bearers, Andrew Gould (Navy), George Tucker (Navy), Chesley
Pittman (Forestry), William Sampson (Forestry), John McLean
(Forestry), John Pittman (Royal Artillery) Abe Pittman (Forestry),
Carl Sheppard (Forestry), Abe Gibbons (Royal Artillery), Herbert
Sheppard (Navy), and Henry Tucker (Navy)

207

Veterans of the North Branch 55 PlumPoint

Front row, Left to Right: John McLean (Forestry), George Chambers (Navy), George Tucker (Navy), Pius Genge (Forestry), and Steve Tucker (Forestry)

Back row, Left to Right: Henry Tucker (Navy), William Sampson (Forestry), Abe Pittman (Forestry), and David Allingham (Forestry)

# BATTLE IN THE STRAITS

The people have fond memories,
Watching from their homestead soil.
It was the Battle of the Atlantic,
Taking place in the Strait of Belle Isle.

It was November one, in forty one,
The German U-boats they numbered four.
They attacked the convoy fifty two,
Between Cook's Harbour and Lanse au Moore.

On November three, the battle raged,
Five ships sunk, so history states.
Many sailors lost their lives,
In the battle in the Straits.

On August twenty seven in the year of forty two,
The U-boat five seventeen was steaming slow,
It spotted the S.S. *Chatham*,
And sent her down below.

Her passengers of five hundred and sixty two,
Thirteen brave souls were lost.
Thus the Battle in the Straits,
Came at a terrible cost.

To the end of the year of forty four,
More ships went down in style.
Until the end of World War Two,
When peace came to the Strait of Belle Isle.

The Author

# WAR IN THE STRAIT OF BELLE ISLE

For the people of the Great Northern Peninsula and Labrador, some of the major battles of the navy occurred right on their doorsteps, and many of the older people from the area can recall watching the fire power of some of these battles light up the skies.

On August 1, 1915, it was reported that a submarine periscope had been sighted near the Gray Islands. On March 15, 1917, the French vessel S.S. *Primaire* was torpedoed and sunk twenty-one miles south-south-east of Belle Isle. Another ship, the S.S. *Thracia* of the cunard lines, was sunk twelve miles north of Belle Isle. On March 25, 1917, the S.S. *Bayard* was torpedoed twenty miles north-west of Belle Isle. On July 4, 1917, the S.S. *Gothland* was torpedoed ten miles south of Belle Isle; twenty-two of the crew drowned. On November 11, 1918, the Armistice was signed and the submarine attack ceased.

Prior to the Second World War the Canadian Government took steps to improve safety along the northern coast by setting up an air reconnaissance between Hamilton Inlet and the Strait of Belle Isle. In January 1940 the RCAF was granted land at Red Bay for a sea plane base. A Newfoundland Ranger was sent north to investigate some suspicious reports from St. Lunaire Bay. He left Corner Brook on the cutter *Shulamit* for St. Anthony via Port Saunders and Flower's Cove. On July 11, they reached St. Lunaire. Later in the day they left St. Anthony for Battle Harbour. They also visited Forteau and Henley Harbour. When they returned to St. Anthony, they proceeded to Cremaillere where a Canadian Naval party was active in Cremaillere Bay. Also at Cook's Harbour, Pisolet Bay and Ha Ha Bay, as well as Quirpon, Griquet and St. Lunaire Bay, the Newfoundland Ranger patrolled the area on the MVS *St. Barbe*.

A search was made of St. Lunaire Bay for the possible sighting of an enemy U-boat. The first U-boat to explore the Strait of Belle Isle in World War II was *U-111*. Early in June 1941, heavy ice prevented the enemy U-boat from penetrating very far into the Strait.

In the fall of 1941, a second wave of four U-boats came to the Strait of Belle Isle. On November 1, 1941, the attacks in the

Strait began with an attack on the convoy SC-52. On November 3, an all out battle was taking place in the Strait of Belle Isle, with the torpedoing and sinking of the S.S. *Gemsbuck*, S.S. *Everoja*, S.S. Rose *Schiaffino*, S.S. *Gretavale*, and the S.S. *Flynder Borg*.

The next wave of U-boats came in 1942. When the U-Boats penetrated the Strait on August 24, the U-boat *513* cruised the coast line from Cape Norman to Cape Bauld. On August 27, the U-boat *517* torpedoed the American Troop Ship S.S. *Chatham*, carrying 562 passengers, thirteen of whom lost their lives.

The survivors were picked up and landed in communities along the coast. On the night of September 1, 1942, the German U-boat *517* entered the harbour at Forteau and came within twenty meters of the wharf. The sub lay on the bottom outside Forteau harbour after encountering a high speed patrol boat. The U-boat *165* then attacked and sank the S.S. *Arlyn* and the American tanker S.S. *Laramie*.

In July 1943, the 4,700 ton HMCS *Preserver* was sent to provide anti-submarine defence in the Strait of Belle Isle. This first anti-submarine patrol was set up to guard the entrance to the Straits. The defence was carried out by the *Trois-Rivieres*. During the 101 days, the "Red Bay Navy" had seen sixteen convoys safely through the Strait of Belle Isle. There were no further enemy U-boats attacks in the Straits until the 1944 October attacks. At the end of World War II, peace returned to the Strait of Belle Isle.

# NOTES TO THE READER

It is literally impossible to write or read about anything pertaining to Northern Newfoundland and coastal Labrador without having to mention the work of the Grenfell Mission. From the time Dr. Grenfell came to our shores in 1892 to the present day, and the war years, especially World War II, and the Battle in the Strait of Belle Isle, where many ships were torpedoed, many lives were both lost and saved. There are people in the areas around Cook's Harbour, Raleigh, Ship Cove and others, who can relate to you today, standing out by their door, or looking through the kitchen window and watching the awesome fire power taking place just a few miles away.

On one particular occasion, a ship had been torpedoed near Belle Isle. A raft, filled with survivors was spotted by an aircraft, which led to a corvette being launched to the scene. When the corvette reached the raft, all of those who were capable were standing up in several inches of water, to make room for those who couldn't stand.

Many of the survivors were in very bad shape, some had swallowed large amounts of oil and were vomiting. They were so coated with oil that their lifebelts had to be cut from them. Some were unconscious, others barely breathing and others very near death due to injuries and exposure.

They were brought to the tiny Grenfell Nursing Station at Forteau where the whole community pitched in to help. The nursing station had just one, two-bed ward, and staffed by one Grenfell nurse and a local girl aid. Some of the healthier survivors went to the homes of the local people. Among the survivors were two cooks and a baker who took over the kitchen and gave the nurse and her aid more time to attend to the sick.

A call went to the large Grenfell hospital in St. Anthony for assistance. Dr. Charles Curtis, who took over for Dr. Grenfell, sent the Grenfell Hospital *Maraval* to Forteau to pick up the more injured and sick survivors and bring them to St. Anthony, all the while under surveillance of German U-boats. As in Forteau, the people of St. Anthony took some of survivors in their homes.

After the War, in 1946, a young doctor came to St. Anthony by the name of Gordon Thomas, who a little later took over as head of the Grenfell Association from retiring Dr. Curtis. The young medical doctor was fresh from the Royal Canadian Army Medical Corps, who during the war, trained young medical students for work on the battlefields. Captain Gordon Thomas was to leave for the battlefront himself when a cease fire was declared. Captain Thomas O.C.M.D. spent thirty-three years administering the sick all along the Great Northern Peninsula and all along the Labrador coast, from the Quebec North shore to Hebron. During these thirty-three years, there were very few Veterans of the North who weren't administered to and helped by this man; following in the footsteps of his two predecessors; Grenfell and Curtis. After both the first World War and the second, many of these veterans found work with the Grenfell Mission, running the hospital ships, on its dry docks, farms, machine shops, and elsewhere. As one veteran told me, "He was the best doctor we ever had."

## THE *MARAVAL*
(The little ship that could)

She was just a little ship,
Maraval, was her name.
A hospital ship that served the coast,
From Harbour Deep to Nain.

There was a battle in the Straits,
A passenger ship had gone down.
The survivors were plucked from a raft,
And taken to Forteau town.

Some were sick and injured,
Some had swallowed a lot of oil.
Many were nearly unconscious,
While other sufferings were mild.

A call went out for assistance.
To the Grenfell Hospital in St. Anthony Town,
Doctor Curtis he sent the *Maraval*,
As the news soon spread around.

Around Belle Isle, she did steam,
Heading for the Forteau town.
All while been spied upon,
By the German U-boats of renown.

The worst of the sick she did take,
To the hospital across the bay,
Some were so coated in oil,
Their life belts had to be cut away.

The little ship had done her work,
She served her country well,
Likewise the men that crewed her,
Including Captain Bill.

The Author

214

## THE LITTLE SHIP THAT WOULD

The Grenfell Hospital Ship *Maraval* was involved in the Battle in the Strait of Belle Isle, World War II. Brought survivors from a torpedoed ship in the Straits from Forteau in Labrador to the Grenfell Hospital in St. Anthony.

Captain Gordon Thomas OC MD
Canadian Medical Corp
World War II

# ABLE SEAMAN 'JUST NUISANCE' – ROYAL NAVY

John A. Bromley – Ex Royal Navy

One of the most unforgettable characters that I had the privilege of knowing during the war was Able Seaman Just Nuisance. He was a sailor who never went to sea, often went AWOL (absent without leave), was often disobedient and slept in on a regular basis. He had good and bad points. But he was seldom punished for his misdeeds.

'Just Nuisance' was a 150 pound Great Dane. He was also a great friend of naval seamen. He lived in the Royal Navy barracks at Simon's Town, South Africa. The sailors treated him to all sorts of tidbits, like pork pieces and beer, gave him daily showers, took him for walks and spoiled him rotten. He considered that all sailors were his friends. He recognized his mates by their bell-bottom trousers, square blue collars and navy hats. Servicemen of a different type uniform were normally given a friendly but definite 'by-pass.' He was exceptionally intelligent and was know to guide tipsy sailors from the train station to their ship, or to the barracks.

I first met Just Nuisance while on shore leave. We were on the train bound for Cape Town, twenty-five miles north of Simon's Town, when suddenly this huge animal barges down the aisle and jumps up on the seat beside me scaring me half to death. When he leaned over and licked me on the face, I wasn't sure if it was a friendly gesture or whether or not he was checking me over for his next meal. The conductor came along and patted him on head, and said to me: "Don't worry, this is Able Seaman Just Nuisance. He's a sailor, just like you." I soon found out that he travelled regularly with his sailor buddies.

There were twenty-seven stops between Simon's Town and Cape Town. He would jump off at just about every station, bound along the platform and hop back on the train at a different compartment. There was no doubt that he had the run of the place.

However it was not always so. Early in 1940, when he first started hitching rides, the train staff were quite annoyed with him. When they did manage to put him off at a station stop, he would wait patiently and board the next one to come along. The rail authorities threatened his owner, a Mr. Chaney, that if he didn't keep him home, they would impound him and have him put down. When the word got out, his sailor mates were furious. Mr. Chaney asked the Port Commander of naval personnel if he could do something as he felt the naval rating was mostly responsible for the dog's behaviour. But he did admit that the dog was "just a darn nuisance."

The Port Commander assured the owner, surprisingly, that he certainly could do something; and he did. They held a special ceremony in the naval drill hall, inducted the Great Dane into the Royal Navy, bestowed on him the name Just Nuisance, with the rank of Able Seaman. He was issued an ID card which entitled him to travel free on all public transportation anywhere in South Africa, like any other naval rating. The problem was solved.

It would take several pages to list everything – good or otherwise – attributed to this noble dog. He became a poster dog for several War Bond drives, as well as being paraded for recruiting programs. Suffice to say that he served his country well in wartime.

In 1944 he was suffering from heart problems, which was slowly paralyzing him. The great hind quarters finally gave out, a result no doubt, of vaulting on and off the liberty trains with his sailor buddies. When he could no longer stand, the Royal Navy decided to put him to sleep. On April 1, 1944 (his 7th birthday), they took him by lorry to the Simon's Town Naval Hospital and put him in one of the beds; pillows, white sheets and all. It is reported that when the Chief Surgeon reached down to remove the sheet for the injection, Just Nuisance opened his eyes, reached up with much effort, and licked the doctor's hand. His eyes closed and the massive head fell back on the pillow, seemingly knowing what awaited him.

Able Seaman Just Nuisance was buried at Camp Klaver, Simon's Town, with full military honours. There was a gun salute, and a bugler played the Last Post. His headstone states: "He was a Great Dane – and a Great Friend."

Able Seaman Just Nuisance
on a Train Ride

Just Nuisance
at the Union Jack Club

Just Nuisance buried with full Military honours

# THE HEAVY ARTILLERY
## 166TH AND 59TH
## WORLD WAR II

They were the soldiers of the North,
One sixty six and fifty nine.
They followed in their father's footsteps,
From Italy to the Rhine.

They fought their way through North Africa,
Likewise on Normandy's beach.
The Battle at Monte Cassino,
Freedom was within their reach.

The fought the battle for Catarelto Ridge,
Likewise at Morrey-En-Bessin.
They fought their way across Europe,
Teaching the enemy a lesson.

They fought along the Gothic Line,
Likewise they crossed the Rhine.
It was a bloody battle they fought,
Leaving many of their comrades behind.

The twenty-five pounder was their gun,
Likewise the seven point two.
The "Long Tom" too was their defence,
Of their soldiers brave and true.

Many of their brave soldiers,
Paid the supreme sacrifice.
While others carry the battle scars,
Which will remain with them for life.

The Author

# NEWFOUNDLANDERS AND LABRADORIANS IN THE BRITISH ARMY
## THE 166TH REGIMENT-ROYAL ARTILLERY
### 1939-1945

When war broke out in 1939, there was an immediate call for Newfoundlanders and Labradorians to enter the Royal Navy. Once this got underway the attention turned to the army. Newfoundland had suffered terrible loses in the Royal Newfoundland Regiment in World War I. This led to the decision to recuit instead, two Heavy Artillery Regiments, the 57th and the 59th Royal Artillery. And on April 14, 1940, the first group of 400 men left Newfoundland for England. By 1940, 1430 Newfoundlanders and Labradorians were in the Royal Artillery from some 200 communities.

While this recruiting was taking place, the "Phony War" in Europe came to an end. On May 22, 210 recruits arrived from Newfoundland. Then came the "Miracle of Dunkirk." From June 4 to June 14, the Naval Forces evacuated nearly 339,000 British and Allied Soldiers with an armada of small boats and warships. On June 7, the third establishment arrived from Newfoundland and the 57th Regiment was at full strength with its own identity as the Newfoundland Heavy Regiment 57.

The 166th Field Regiment was formed in 1940. It was not officially born until July 28, 1941, after the change over from the 57th, including Newfoundland officers. By the end of 1941, fourteen of the NCOs were Newfoundlanders and a good portion of the officers.

In November 1941, the 166th went to Larkhill to train in Field Artillery. This Newfoundland Regiment, like their forefathers in World War I, found great hospitality in Scotland. Newfoundlanders were welcomed everywhere. On January 20, 1942, sixteen men from the Regiment left for overseas. On February 1, 1943, they entered Algiers where they were transferred for the 300-mile journey to Bone, on the North African Coast, where they would be involved in "Operation Torch." The 166th Field Regiment and a number of six-pounder anti-tank guns soon became involved in the assault.

The 166th was assigned to support three French Battalions, the 29th Regiment Des Tiraulleurs Algeriens, three Battalions of the 7th Regiment Des Tiraulleurs Algeriens, and the 11th Battalion De Goums. Observation Post System (OPS) was the most dangerous aspect of Field Artillery. The Newfoundlanders quickly came to good terms with the French troops although there was some difficulty with the language.

On April 7, 1943, the first Newfoundland soldier was killed in World War II. From April 9 to 12 seven men were wounded and on the 12th two were killed. On April 18, the Regiment received orders to move north to the area of Medjez-el-Bab. Before they reached it, three more men would be killed.

They settled in an area near Longstop Hill which was still occupied by the enemy. The area was full of land mines and five more of the Regiment men lost their lives when an ammunition truck was blown up by a mine.

A big battle was underway to push the Germans and Italians out of North Africa. The 166th Regiment was assigned to support the 5th Corps. The attack started on April 22 at Longstop Hill. At 10 p.m. the Artillery barrage started and continued until 2 a.m. Their 158 field guns medium and heavy, fired concentrations in front of the 78th Division's attack. At 2 a.m. the Regiment moved its guns to support the 24th Guards Brigade, which was attacking two hills northeast of Madjez. It was a long and arduous day and the 166th along with other regiments kept up a constant fire as they slowly fought their way forward. As they moved ahead, two more Newfoundlanders lost their lives. By 10 p.m. they had fired over 7000 rounds.

The next day the battle raged on, and the 23rd, the Highland Division, gained the top of the ridge with heavy casualties. The Newfoundlanders were in the thick of the fight, setting up observation posts under heavy fire, and over mined territory. A German tank regiment attacked them, one was killed and two OPS members were wounded.

The Regiment moved on to support the infantry with more casualties. May 13 was an unlucky day for the Regiment. "E" and "F" troops came under heavy fire near Bir Meherga and three members of the Number 1 gun crew were killed and three wounded.

On May 13 the Tunisian campaign reached a victorious conclusion for the allies. On May 20 the 166th Regiment took part in a great victory parade in Tunis. On June 21 the Regiment moved back across Algeria almost as far as Tripoli about 600 miles in scorching heat and terrible road conditions. As one gunner wrote, "We travelled 1,100 miles to move 110 yards." They stayed for three months. Twenty-four of their members would be left behind in different cemeteries.

The 166th Regiment stayed in North Africa until October 8, where they sailed for Italy. They arrived in Taranto, Italy, on October 2, where they supported the 17th Indian Brigade in a successful attack on Furci.

In the battle for the Sangro, the Regiment had hard going. In December, the Regiment moved across the Sangro to the Moro River. They moved to support the Canadian Regiment in taking Ortona in which four members were killed and five wounded. By December 1943, thirty-three men had been killed. On January 31, 1944, the 166th received orders to move across the Italian Peninsula. On February 26, 1944, the 166th dug in their guns facing Monte Cassino. During this encounter, three more men died in the line of duty and several were badly wounded.

Early in April 1944, the 166th returned to the Adriatic Front, near Orsogna, where the Regiment suffered more casualties. The Regiment moved near Prato, for an assault on Mount Catarelto, where they suffered more casualties in the Battle of Catarelto Ridge. They were successful in capturing the ridge after three days of heavy fighting.

On February 24, 1945, the first men of the 166th Royal Artillery Regiment started leaving for home and the Regiment was placed in reserve. This was the end for the 166th Regiment in World War II.

They fought a bitter campaign and did an outstanding job. They would leave behind forty-eight of their members and many more would bear the physical and mental scars for the rest of their lives. We have been reminded of just some of the battles of the 166th regiment in World War II. There are many more heroes out there, whom history has not recorded. The 166th Regiment R.A. carried out its duties well and made the difference in "Holding the Line."

## HERE ARE THE FACES OF SOME OF THE VETERANS OF THE NORTH WHO FOUGHT IN THESE BLOODY BATTLES.

Abraham (Abe) Gibbons
Plum Point
166th Regiment-Royal Artillery
World War II
"Clem was my buddy, he saved
my life."

Clemence (Clem) Barrett
Cook's Harbour
166th Regiment-Royal Artillery
World War II

# THIS WORLD OF LOVE AND HATE
## By an Unknown Soldier

There's a broken, battered graveyard
Somewhere up behind our lines
Where there's many a lifeless body
That were one-time friends of mine.

I remember how we reached them,
Dripped in sweat and all forlorn,
For to give a decent burial
To their bodies their souls had worn.

Though the shells are bursting around us,
We still listen to the roar
Of the guns we answer back with
Like big breakers on the shore.

Then up comes one of our comrades
When the day was growing late,
Would you please come bury another
One who used to be my mate.

So we went out in the darkness
To a body lying there,
Just a heap shone in the twilight
And with reverence said a prayer.

Then the padre watched our faces,
As he read the service through
From "I am the Resurrection"
To the last, the great adieu.

There are many kinds of sorrow
In the world of love and hate,
But there is no greater sorrow
Than a soldier for his mate.

# NUNATSUAMI NALLINIK PIUNGISAUTINILLU

SiKumisimajumik, siKuttitausimajumik minguisipviKavuk
Nanikiak akunnitini
Unuttuit omangituit timet
Ilannagisimajakka.

IkKaumavunga Kanuk tigulaummanganni,
Kitjijajut Kimainnatausimajut
Iluvitautsiagialet
Timingit inosingit nungusimahjut.

Kukiutsuat Kukiajut sanittini,
NalaKattajavut pipvalanningit
Kukiutinut akiniaKattajavut
Sollu ingiulivatsuat sitsami.

Ilavut tikiniadlutik
Ulluk najilittilugu unnusami,
IluvitsigiattugajakKen ilattinik
UnatapvimeKatigilauttaganik.

Taimaimmat unnauakut ainiadluta
Timimmut tamanetuinnajumut
Kaulitainnatillugu
Gude-mut tutsiadluta

Ilavut kenattinik takunnajut,
Atuatsiluni tutsianikkut
Allatausimajumit "Uvanga Inuggutauvunga Makitjutaulungalu"
Naninganut, angijumik atsunai.

Unuttunik kitsanattuKavuk
Nunatsuami nallinikkut piungusaannikullu,
Tavatauk anginitsamik kitsanattuKangilak
Sutjututsatut ilangatalu.

William Willette
Winterhouse Brook
166th Regiment Royal Artillery
World War II

Herbert Reardon
Goose Cove
Royal Artillery
World War II

British Infantry (166th Regiment) advancing through the ruins of Cassino, Italy

Photograph courtesy of Imperial War Museum, London, NA 14999

Stephen Tucker
St. Anthony
166th Regiment-Royal Artillery
World War II
Fought in North Africa and in the Bloody Battle of Monte Cassino,
Italy

George Williams
Current Island
Royal Artillery
World War II

The twenty-five pounder of the Newfoundland 166th
Regiment-Royal Artillery in action in Italy, World War II

The 166th, in the battle of Monte Cassino, Italy, 1944

Stephen Tucker
St. Anthony
166th Regiment
Royal Artillery
World War II

A friend of war stricken children of Cassino, Italy

Mazzagrognia, Italy, showing the scars of Battle, 1944

Soldier of the 166th Regiment repairing vehicle in the Front
Line Cancello, Italy, 1944

# THE 59TH NEWFOUNDLAND HEAVY REGIMENT
## ROYAL ARTILLERY
## 1939-1945

This Regiment came into existence June 15, 1940. On July 6, 1940, the first group of the 59th went overseas and lost its first man in an air raid in London in 1941. On December 19 another wave of ninety-six men arrived from Newfoundland.

Early in 1943 the 59th Regiment became a part of the 3rd AGRA (Army Group Royal Artillery). On July 6, 1944, at 08:15 the 59th fired their first rounds at the enemy at Caen-Bayeaux Road.

By July 9 most of Caen was in Allied hands and the 59th advanced to positions at Norreyen Bessen, west of Caen, where it was the job of the regiment to put enemy artillery out of action. On July 17, they were attacked and one officer and eleven men were wounded. A few days later the 59th Regiment lost its first man in the Normandy Campaign.

In August the 59th Regiment moved to Ste-Honorine-De-Fay. In a week of bloody fighting, the assault moved forward. On August 15, the 59th crossed the Orne and on the 18th they were at Norton L' Abbaye northwest of Falaise. This advance resulted in massive artillery fire leading to an enemy surrender.

On August 3, the 23rd Battery of the 59th Regiment crossed the Seine supporting the 12th Corps of the British Army. On September 7, they came into action near Ghent. On September 22, the Battery crossed the Meuse-Escaut Canal and Holland Canal, going into action west of Eindhoven. At Eindhoven the Regiment spent days bringing down as much fire as possible on the enemy. On September 25, they moved toward Belgium clearing the enemy out of Scheldt estuary using their "Long Toms," which had a range of 25,000 yards.

The Regiment was also involved in bitter fighting at Breskens Pocket. The Newfoundlanders' first job was long range shelling of German ships in Flushing Harbour, where they scored some direct hits. For the next five weeks, Newfoundland gunners would be in action day and night, capturing all the enemy positions remaining in Belgium and Holland. When the battle was won, the

Regiment was congratulated on a job "well done," stating that, "The island may well raise to a pinnacle of pride among the highest tradition of its history."

On October 6 the Newfoundland gunners were engaged in the work of eliminating enemy batteries in the northern part of the pocket, especially the big coastal guns west of Breskens. They faced murderous rifle and machine gun fire from the German division entrenched in the dikes. It took four days of heavy casualties before they established a bridgehead on the north bank of the canal.

The 59th moved to a new location near Scheldt in an area known as South Beveland where it was involved in five days of heavy shelling. They then moved and captured "Fortress Island" of Walcheren.

On November 6 the Regiment moved across Belgium. On November 14 to 16, the massive bombardment kept up. It was reported that 200 shells were fired every minute. The Newfoundlanders moved to Helthuizen near the banks of the Maas where they opened fire. It was the first time artillery shells had landed on German soil during the War; victory was in the air.

By January 21, 1945, a long-cherished ambition was realized when the 23rd Battery went into action on German soil, near Hongen. Another Battery of the Regiment went into action in the Roer Triangle because there were no armoured tanks. The Newfoundland gunners were being asked to play a big part in the war.

For the 59th, the task of moving big guns and equipment in terrible condition was arduous. On February 16, 1945, two members of the 59th were killed. Two more were trapped in a minefield, but in pouring rain and pitch darkness they were rescued.

The Regiment was firing in support of the 1st Canadian Army operations on February 8. Here there would be a volume of shells employed unequalled on any front during World War II. More than 1000 guns had been assembled for this offensive and the barrage was awesome. The 22nd Battery recorded firing 1000 of its 200-pound shells.

On February 26, 1945, the Newfoundlanders were involved near Maas and the town of Goch, which they had taken earlier in the war. They bombarded German points on the other side of the Rhine, until March 15 when they were moved to a position near

Sonsbech where they were given the job of destroying German observation posts.

On the evening of March 27, 1945, the 59th Regiment rumbled across the Rhine on a pontoon bridge. Nearly a quarter of a million Germans were trapped in the "Ruhr Pocket." On April 11, the 59th moved to an area west of the Weser, the town of Verden was taken, and on the 19th the Newfoundlanders and Labradorians crossed the Wester to go into action near the city of Bremen. By nightfall on the 29th, a firm bridgehead over the Elbe was established.

On May 2, 1945, the Regiment moved to the left bank of the Elbe about fifteen miles from Hamburg. The next day Hamburg surrendered and the guns went silent. A cease-fire went into effect on May 5, 1945.

On July 5, 1945, the 59th left Bergendarf for England exactly one year after they had landed. They had been tried and tested through a year of action. They left behind nine comrades who had died in the line of duty on the Continent, bringing the Regiment losses to twenty-four. In leaving, their Commanding Officer said, "If there is any job requiring courage, determination, and hard work, these men will do it if it is in the bounds of human endeavour."

There are others who payed a price in this freedom, but this information is hard to come by. These are the many Newfoundlanders who served with the Canadian Army and other units of the British Army, as well as the many young Newfoundlanders who joined the Forestry Corps. There were also 190 young women who joined the Canadian Women's Army Corps, giving a total of approximately 2700 young Newfoundlanders and Labradorians in the ranks of the Army during World War II.

## THE BEACHES OF NORMANDY

After landing on the Beaches of Normandy, the soldiers of the 59th Newfoundland Heavy Regiment proceeded inland. As one Newfoundland soldiers remarked, "I'll never forget the sight of a soldier's grave, by the side of the road. It wasn't a neat little cross, but the piece of a rifle and a helmet with the camouflage netting still attacked. No name was visible. A jeep drove down the road and in it was a man who took off his black beret with two badges in it. He waved his beret. The man was General Montgomery."

For three nights the German reconnaissance planes took photographs of the Newfoundland Battery site at Norrey-En-Bessen. On the night of July 17th, 1944 the enemy dropped flares on the Newfoundland positions, lighting up the area like noonday. Then the attack began and the first bomb hit an ammunition dump, which turned the place into a 'living hell,' with bombs and shells exploding all over the place. Thirteen Newfoundlanders and Labradorians were wounded in the battle.

*"My most vivid memory is of a soldier caught in wire on the beach. I knelt beside him and discovered he'd bled to death. Beside him was a pack of cigarettes that was opened with one cigarette hanging out. Beside it was a lighter. I tried it but it was clogged. The poor man had been trying to have one last smoke and the lighter hadn't worked. Nothing had worked for him that day."*

A WORLD WAR II VETERAN

# SINCE I MET YOU I'M NOT AFRAID
## BY AN UNKNOWN SOLDIER

Look God, I have never spoken to you.
But now I want to say "How do you do?"
You see God, they told me you didn't exist.
And like a fool I believed all this.

Last night from a shell hole, I saw your sky,
I figured right then they had told me a lie.
Had I taken time to see things you made.
I'd had known they weren't calling a spade a spade.

I wonder God, if you'd shake my hand.
Some how I feel that you'd understand.
Funny I had to come to this hellish place,
Before I had time to see your face.

Well I guess there isn't much more to say,
But I'm sure glad God that I met you today.
I guess that zero will soon be here,
But I'm not afraid, since I know you're near.

The signal, well, God, I have to go.
I like you lots, this I want you to know.
Look now! This will be a horrible fight,
Who knows? I may come to your house tonight.

Though I wasn't friendly to you before,
I wonder God if you'd wait at your door.
Look I'm crying!! Me shedding tears!
I wish I had known you these many years.

Well I have to go now God, good-bye.
Strange since I met you I'm not afraid to die.

# TAKULAUGAKKINIT KAPPIASUGUNNAIKUNGA

Takugit Gude, nilliutilautsimangilagit
Tavatualli mannaulittuk uKautigumalikKagit "Kanuivet".
Gude, uKautijaulaugama sakKijangitutit.
IsumaKatsiangitutut tamanna ukpiginiadlugu.

Unnuagulauttumi ititsamedlunga, Kiait takulaukKaga,
Kaujiniadlunga taikkua uvannik salluKitsisimahjut.
PivitisaKalauguma takullunga sanasimajannik
KaujimagajalaukKunga, puaggitik sipengungituk

Gude apigivagit, tigulittugajakKama.
Kanukkiak ikpiniavunga tukisiniattutit,
Tamaugalugaska iniutsiangitumut aigiaKannigama
Kenannik takukKanaga.

UkausitsaKatsiagunnaigama,
KusiasummagikKunga Gude ullumi takukKaugakkit.
ImmaKa ulluk najinitsaga tikilikKuk,
Kappiasungilanga, Kaujimagama saniganejutit.

Nalunaititsivuk! Gude, aullagiaKalikKunga
Angijumik piugivagit, tamanna ilinnut KaujimajaukKujaga.
Takugit! Tamanna kappianattuk pinnianiuniakKuk,
Kina Kaujimava? Unnuak KainiakKunga.

Inotsialaungikaluadlunga ilinnut sivungani
Kaujigumavunga utakKigajammangappit ukkuani.

Takugit KialikKunga!! Kupvika katagajut!
Kanuttovunga akuninit ilinnik Kaujimajutsaulauttunga.

AullagiaKalikKunga Gude, atsunai
Taimanganit takulaugakkinit kappiasugunnaiKunga
tuKungiamik.

Norman Lance Patey
St. Anthony
59th Newfoundland Heavy Regiment
World War II

"About 500 German Bombers attacked our battery at 600 feet and showered bombs on us. There were holes in the ground large enough to put houses. One bomb landed about three feet from me. That was the one that got me. I was hospitalized with wounds with the option to return home, but decided to stay and help my comrades."

Roy Young
Birchy Head
59th Newfoundland Heavy
Regiment
World War II

Samuel Hatcher
Winter House Brook
59th Newfoundland Heavy
Regiment
World War II

Albert Peter Letto
L'Anse au Clair
Across Europe with the 59th Newfoundland Heavy Regiment
Royal Artillery
World War II

"We were glad when they told us the war was over, but sad that
some of our comrades wouldn't be going home with us."

# THE DYING SOLDIER

## E. Sparrow

Under the sunny skies of France,
    He yielded up his life.
The fisher lad,
    from Newfoundland
Unused to war and strife.

And e'er his dying eyes were closed,
    He saw, as in a dream;
The tall grey cliff,
    the haven where
The home lights softly gleam.

He saw his boat at anchor lie,
    He saw his comrades true,
He heard again,
    the songs he loved,
The songs his childhood knew.

Across the din of war, he heard
    The waves break on the strand,
And his heart went back,
    in the last hour,
To far off Newfoundland.

7.2 inch Howitzer used by the 59th Heavy Regiment in Normandy

155-mm "Long Tom" used by the 59th Heavy Regiment during World War II

British Troops (59th Regiment) landing on the Beaches of Normandy, June 1944

Courtesy Imperial War Museum, London, B 5103

# THE AIR WAR
## WORLD WAR I
### AND
## WORLD WAR II

They flew into the heavens above,
Over the battlefields below.
Many of them gave their lives,
For the freedom we now know.

They flew the Halifax Bombers,
Also the Spitfire of great fame.
The Mosquitoes and the Liberators,
The air war it was no game.

They fought in the skies over India,
Likewise over Germany too.
They flew in the Battle of Dunkirk,
These airmen so brave and true.

Many of them did not return,
Their land they would see no more.
Many of them lie in unmarked graves,
Others lie in peace on the ocean's floor.

The loss of airmen in World War Two,
Was seventy thousand and even more.
Twenty three thousand were wounded,
Thirty thousand were prisoners of war.

They too paid a price for freedom,
Just like their comrades far below.
May we never ever forget,
Why there are crosses row and row.

The Author

# NEWFOUNDLANDERS AND LABRADORIANS IN THE R.A.F. AND R.C.A.F.
## 1939-1945

During World War II, it was probably impossible to find any branch of the military forces which didn't have a Newfoundland member. The Air Force was no exception. In 1939 a small group of Newfoundlanders went to England and joined the Royal Air Force, many of them finding space on paper carrier ships from Newfoundland to England. Others enlisted in the Forestry Corps but later joined the Royal Air Force.

By 1940, 284 Newfoundlanders were serving in the Royal Air Force. By the end of 1940, 144 Air Force recruits from Newfoundland were training in Canada with the R.C.A.F. and the R.A.F. In 1941 the first recruits arrived in England. The Newfoundland 125th squadron was formed and later other countries became part of it. Thus, it truly became an International Newfoundland Squadron.

Newfoundlanders flew many different types of airplanes including fighter planes such as Spitfires, Mosquitoes, Hurricanes, Beauforts and Beau Fighters. In the Battle of Britain they flew Swordfish, Torpedo Planes, Liberators, Sunderlands, and Catalina Flying Boats. In the bomber command they flew Blenheims, Halifaxs, and Lancasters. They flew in support of the British Army as Hitler invaded France and during the evacuation of Dunkirk. They were part of the crews of the bombers in the attack against Germany, and they served in North Africa in the great battle against the "Desert Fox", General Rommel.

They served in Singapore, the East Indies and Burma and were involved in the great landings of North Africa, Sicily, Italy and Malta. They flew in the ill-fated raid on Dieppe and in the Normandy invasion. They were also involved in the battle to sink the *Bismark*. By December 17, 1941, fifteen Newfoundlanders died while serving with the R.A.F. and R.C.A.F.

Many Newfoundlanders served outside the 125th squadron, besides serving in Britain. They served in many other places all over the world. In 1942-1943, ninety-four young Newfoundlanders in the R.A.F. paid the price for victory. By the time of the Normandy invasion, the 125th squadron had destroyed thirty-seven enemy planes.

The first Newfoundland airman to die in World War II came in 1939. He was flying a bomber in a raid over Bremen; many of these Newfoundland flyers became Air Aces.

These figures show the price paid for peace by so many air-crews throughout the world in World War II, Commonwealth Airmen. 70,250 killed, 23,000 wounded, 13,000 taken prisoners. Nearly 18,000 Canadian Airmen lost their lives in World War II; all for the cause of freedom.

There were 734 Newfoundlanders and Labradorians who served in the Royal Air Force and the Royal Canadian Air Force as Air Crews of which 188 were killed for a loss ratio of thirty-four percent. Of the first fifty-two potential R.A.F. Aircrews that left Newfoundland on August 20, 1940, forty-seven graduated and went overseas. Of these, 25 did not survive the war, for a loss ratio of fifty-five percent. Newfoundlanders who fought in the Air War were not without honours. Twenty-six received Distinguished Flying Medals: two Air Force Crosses; two Air Force Medals; one Croix de Guerre with Gold Star; and six Mentions in Dispatches.

Sergeant George McDonald
Englee
Wireless Operator/Air Tail Gunner
160 Squadron Royal Air Force

Their Liberator Bomber Mark III, FK-239, took off from its base at R.A.F. Sigiriya in Ceylon (Sri Lanka). At 03:00 hours on August 24, 1943, the Bomber was last heard from seventy miles off Ceylon. It is presumed the Bomber crashed into the sea, taking with it its eight crewmembers, including Sergeant George McDonald of Englee.

R.A.F. Halifax Bomber
Over Germany 1944

Photograph courtesy Imperial War Museum, London, C 4713

1827113 Sergeant John Anley Dumaresque
Forteau, Labrador
622 Squadron, Royal Air Force (Volunteer Reserve)
Killed in Action September 20, 1944, age 28 years
Buried in Cambridge Cemetery, U.K., Grave No. 15948

Howard Harvey Hoddinott
Brig Bay
Royal Air Force, World War II

Shot down over Germany on his first mission and taken prisoner

Arthur Boyd
St. Anthony
Royal Air Force, World War II

Ronald Fitzgerald
Conche
Royal Air Force
World War II

Donald Rowsell
Englee
Royal Air Force
World War II

Donald Patey
St. Anthony
Royal Air Force
World War II

Curling Laing
Norris Point
Royal Air Force
World War II

Donald Patey, St. Anthony, with two unidentified aircrew comrades

Pte. Emmanuel David Letto
L'Anse Au Clair
Northern Nova Scotia
Highlanders
World War II
Killed in Action
September 29, 1944

Pte. Emmanuel Letto
Canadian War Cemetery
Callas, France

Private Emmanuel Letto took part in the Battle of Normandy and was involved in the capture of Cap Gris Nez. On September 29, 1944, the Novas and M.L.T. were ordered to destroy the two cross channel batteries at Haringzelles and Franzelle. Unfortunately they ran into some trouble and Private Letto and four of his comrades were killed.

Stella Parsons
Griquet
Canadian Army Corps
World War II

Nora Noseworthy
Green Island Brook
Canadian Medical Corps
World War II

# FORESTRY UNIT
## WORLD WAR I
### AND
## WORLD WAR II

Armed only with a bucksaw,
An axe and a file.
They too helped gained our freedom,
With hard work, sweat and toil.

Their first winter in the Scottish land,
Accommodations were very poor.
Many of them became sick and died,
Far away on the Scottish Shore.

Beans and bologna for breakfast,
To start off a working day.
Eggs were rationed to one per month,
And for fresh meat, twenty-seven cents you pay.

They cut the timber and pitprop,
Bridges for to build.
For walls in the fighting trenches
To protect them from the falling shells.

The Forestry men contributed much,
To the peace in our fair land.
But it took so long for recognition,
These men of the timber stand.

The Author

# THE NEWFOUNDLAND FORESTRY UNIT

Another group of Veterans who helped bring about the peace we enjoy today are those who served overseas with the Forestry Unit. During the Second World War, thirty-four of these members died as a result of accidents or illnesses while serving in the British Isles. Another 335 members of the unit were repatriated back to Newfoundland due to illness.

On November 9, 1939, the Governor of Newfoundland received word that there was a dire need for labourers from Newfoundland for the purpose of cutting pitprops. Those who enlisted agreed to stay for at least six months. They were to be paid approximately the wage paid to loggers who worked for the logging companies back home in Newfoundland, $2.00 per day or $12.00 per week. They agreed to have one dollar a day sent back home to their families. They were to be paid half pay for any days lost due to sickness or injury. All clothing and footwear were to be paid for by the loggers. Pay began on the first day they left home.

The logging camps were somewhat like those back home used by the logging companies. They consisted of a cookhouse, bunkhouse, washroom, forepeak used for offices, plus a few other smaller buildings. The lighting in the camps for the first part of the war years consisted of something similar to that used back home in homes that didn't have electricity; which were most homes in Newfoundland. It was a lantern called the "Tilley" back home. The company who put the lamp on the market ran an ad on the radio which read, "Buy a Tilley, the lamp which lights the island."

The menu in the Forestry Logging Camps was similar to that in the logging camps back home: beans, salt beef, salt pork, salt fish, bologna and hard bread, and staple foods such as sugar, butter, cheese and bacon. Fresh meats and eggs were rationed to one a month. Fresh meat was valued at twenty-seven cents per person per week, with sugar rationed to eight ounces, butter four ounces and bacon two ounces. The only items in plentiful supply were bread, milk, vegetables and, of course, oatmeal (rolled oats) and wild game.

During 1939, the first camps were constructed. Conditions were damp and unsanitary and, as a result, many of the men became sick with influenza resulting in the death of the first two men in the Forestry Unit. Things improved as more camps were constructed. By the time the first six months of the contract came, over 500 of the Forestry Unit decided to leave and enlist in other forces, such as the Royal Navy, Air Force and Army. As a result, an urgent request had to be sent to Newfoundland for more recruits to work in the Forestry Unit.

During the War and even after, there were a lot of people who didn't realize the part the Forestry Unit played in achieving the world peace which was won. However, those countries which were involved in the war did value the service they gave for the cause of freedom. Unfortunately, it took years and even decades for the government and those in authority to finally say, "They also served."

As we look back now we ask ourselves, "Did these men, armed only with a bucksaw, axe and brute strength, really make a difference in winning the wars?" Only history can answer this question, but we all should agree that if not for the pitprops and timber which these men supplied to the allies, it would have been much more difficult gaining access to the enemy line and, more importantly, providing shelter from enemy attacks.

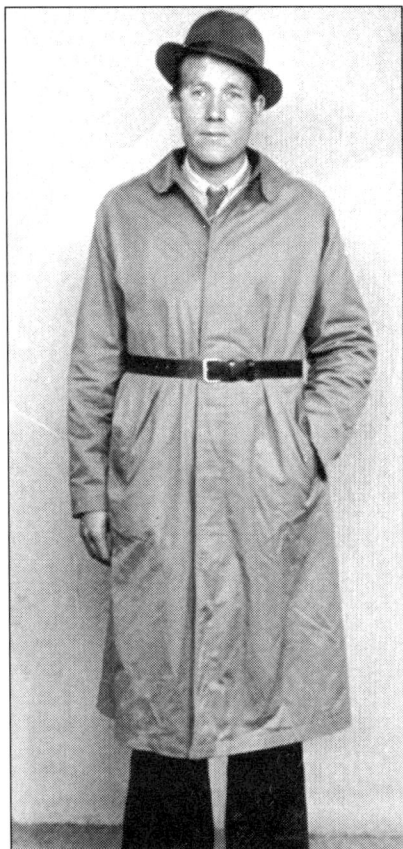

Simon Raymond Hancock
Englee
Forestry Unit
World War II

Headstone of
Simon Raymond Hancock

*Erected by fellow workers*

Died while trying to rescue a drowning worker, June 1940

Leo Lewis
Conche
Forestry Unit
World War II

Michael Byrne
Conche
Forestry Unit
World War II

Henry Doyle
New Ferolle
Forestry Unit
World War II

(BROTHER)

James Doyle
New Ferolle
Forestry Unit
World War II

William Ploughman
Port Saunders
Forestry Unit
World War II

Arthur Hinks
Port Saunders
Forestry Unit
World War II

Left to Right: Stanley Reeves, Englee; Simon Hancock, Englee;
and William Sutton, Roddickton
Forestry Unit
World War II

Simon Hancock and
Stanley Reeves
Forestry Unit
World War II

Edward Myers
Bartlett's Harbour
Forestry Unit
World War II

Cyril Chambers
Bear Cove
Forestry Unit
World War II

Ben "Lee" Fennimore
St. Anthony
Forestry Unit
World War II

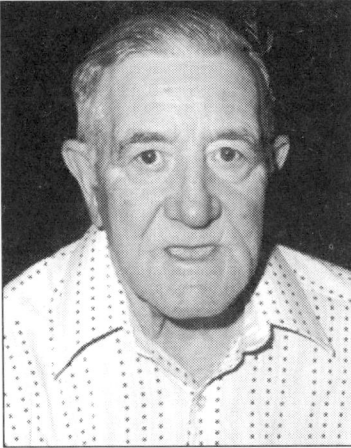

Darius (Roy) Way
Savage Cove
Forestry Unit
World War II

Malcolm Mitchelmore
St. Anthony
Forestry Unit
World War II

Archabold Andrews
St. Anthony
Forestry Unit
World War II

Roland Roberts
St. Anthony
Forestry Unit
World War II

Richard Way
Savage Cove
Forestry Unit
World War II

Henry T. Way
Savage Cove
Forestry Unit
World War II

Isaac Patey
River of Ponds
Forestry Unit
World War I

Unidentified
Forestry Unit
World War I

Caleb Genge
Anchor Point
Forestry Unit
World War II

George Gould
Bear Cove
Forestry Unit
World War II

Michael Breen
Canada Harbour
Forestry, Home Guard
World War II

Shem Newman
Englee
Forestry, Home Guard
World War II

Benjamin Toope
Current Island
Forestry Unit
World War II

Samuel White
Red Bay
Forestry Unit
World War II

Samuel Hodge
Savage Cove
Forestry Unit
World War II

Garland Colbourne
St. Anthony
Forestry Unit
World War II

John Hodge
Savage Cove
Forestry Unit
World War II

Stephen Way
Savage Cove
Forestry Unit
World War II

THEY WERE ARMED ONLY WITH A BUCKSAW AND AXE, YET THE CONTRIBUTION THESE FORESTRY VETERANS MADE TO WORLD PEACE WAS FAR GREATER THAN MANY REALIZED. THEY WERE SUBJECTED TO DEPLORABLE LIVING CONDITIONS, ESPECIALLY IN THE FIRST YEAR, AND THE CONSTANT THREAT OF BOMBING AND SHELLING FROM THE ENEMY.

Forestry Veterans, World War II

Left to Right: William Sampson, Brig Bay; Abraham Chambers, Bear Cove; and Chesley Sampson, Plum Point.

# MERCHANT NAVY
## WORLD WAR I
### AND
## WORLD WAR II

It took years to finally agree,
That they too the criteria did meet.
And be recognized as Veterans,
These brave men of the Merchant Fleet.

Their ships were sunk in the cold Atlantic,
These tough and fearless men.
It was Winston Churchill who said of them,
With dogged determination they went to sea
again.

They carried the food for the Allied forces,
Guns and ammunition their needs to meet.
Timber to build the bridges,
These brave men of the Merchant fleet.

In the Merchant Navy Book of Memory,
Contains three hundred names and more.
Of those who paid the supreme sacrifice,
On a far and distant shore.

In the words of Winston Churchill,
They gave what was in their power.
To gain the victory that we won,
This was their finest hour.

The Author

# NEWFOUNDLANDERS AND LABRADORIANS
## IN THE WAR AT SEA
### THE MERCHANT NAVY
## 1939-1945

The men of the British Merchant Navy, the American Merchant Marine and the Canadian Merchant Navy, were the largely forgotten heroes of what was the longest, as well as one of the bitterest and most costly campaigns of the Second World War. They suffered their first casualties on the day war was declared, September 3, 1939, and their last on May 7, 1945, the eve of VE Day.

In the years between, over 60,000 souls of the Allied Merchant Services lost their lives to Axis torpedoes, bombs and guns, and to the ever present enemy — the weather. Their contribution was a vital one. Without their sacrifice, Britain could not have survived the early years of the war, Russia could not have been supplied with the weapons and raw materials which enabled her to stem and turn the tide of the German invasion, the Mediterranean would have become the mare nostrum of which Mussolini dreamed, and the great seaborn invasions which rolled back the Axis Forces, first in North Africa, and then in Europe and the Pacific, could never had been mounted.

They played a big part in getting supplies across the Atlantic to the countries involved in World War II. They carried food supplies for the soldiers fighting the war: arms, ammunition, fuels for transport equipment, and military equipment including planes and spare parts. All of these were vital materials if any country ever hoped to win a war.

Many of these merchant ships were sunk during the war. This was especially true in the "Battle of the Atlantic" where over 2,000 ships were lost. Approximately 10,000 Newfoundlanders and Labradorians served in the Allied Merchant Navy as well as 12,000 Canadians. Some 334 Newfoundlanders and Labradorians died while serving in the Merchant Navy during World War II. Under the Red Ensign of the British Merchant Navy, 20,000 were lost.

Just a gunshot from the centre of the "Compass Rose", displayed on this memorial, lies a graveyard. It begins there and circles the globe. It is the graveyard of ships and sailors of all nations.

# MERCHANT NAVY MEN

## BY Captain A.W. Caulderwood

You have seen him on the street,
Rolling around on foggy feet.
You have seen him clutch a lamppost for support,
You have seen him arm in arm,
With a maid of doubtful charm,
Who was leading Johnny safely back to port.

You have shuddered in disgust,
As he sometimes bites the dust.
You've ignored him when you've seen him on a spree,
But you've never seen the rip,
Of his dark and lonely ship,
Pushing furrows through a sub-infested sea.

You have cheered our naval lads,
In their sally iron clads.
You have spared a cheer for infantrymen too,
You have shuttered in a funk,
When you read "Big Mail Boat Sunk,"
Did you ever give a thought about the crew?

Yet he brings the wounded home,
Through a mine-infested zone.
And he ferries all the troops across at night,
He belongs to no brigade,
He's neglected, underpaid,
But he's always in the thickest of the fight.

And he fights the lurking Hun,
With his ancient four inch gun.
And he'll ruin Aldoph Hitler's little plan,
He's a hero, he's a nut,
He's the bloody limited-but,
He just another Merchant Navy man.

Charles (Charlie) Simms
St. Anthony
Merchant Navy
World War II

Richard (Dick) Richards
Little Brehat
Merchant Navy
World War I

Richard Patey
Great Brehat
Merchant Navy
World War I

Richard (Dick) Simms
St. Anthony
Merchant Navy
World War II

# Korean War

## 1950-1953

# LEST WE FORGET

Canadians
Korean War
1950-1953
Enlisted
26,791

Fatal & non Fatal Battle Casualties
1,558
Killed in Action
516

A soldier of the Royal Canadian Regiment awaiting medical aid
after night patrol, June 1952

# KOREA
## 1950-1953

They were the first Newfoundland Canadians,
To fight in a declared war.
They fought in the land called Korea,
Far away from their native shore.

They fought at little Gibraltar,
On hill three fifty-five.
They fought in the rice paddies,
Some would lose their lives.

They fought across the thirty-eight parallel,
From the mountains of Kakhul-Bong.
Many young soldiers were killed,
Their bodies lie in peace in Pusan.

They fought under the United Nations,
In a war that was hard to win.
The terrain was rough and rugged,
They were the toughest of Canada's men.

After the war ended in the year fifty three,
After they had taken their stand.
Some returned to the land they loved,
Others rest in peace in the yard of Pusan.

The Author

# NEWFOUNDLANDERS IN THE KOREAN WAR
## 1950 – 1953

The first war Newfoundlanders and Labradorians fought in after becoming Canadians was the Korean War. On June 25, 1950, the forces of North Korea crossed the 39th Parallel into the Republic of Korea. This marked the beginning of hostilities which were to rage for three full years in the hills, swamps and rice paddies. Canada's contribution was only exceeded by that of the United States and Great Britain. Canada demonstrated her willingness to uphold the United Nations ideals and to take up arms in support of peace and freedom. Canada's newest subjects, Newfoundlanders and Labradorians, were a part of the Canadian force. Many of them served in Korea; some remain there in the United Nation Memorial Cemetery in Pusan and probably other places after paying the supreme sacrifice for world peace.

All tolled, 26,791 Canadians served in the Korean War, and another 7,000 served in the theatre between the cease-fire and the end of 1955. Canadian casualties were 516 in the hard fought war.

The first Canadian aid to the UN Forces came from the Royal Canadian Navy. On July 12, 1950, three Canadian Destroyers, HMCS *Cayuga*, HMCS *Athabaskan* and HMCS *Sioux* were dispatched to Korean waters to serve under the United Nations command. Also in July, a Royal Canadian Air Force Squadron was assigned to the area. Number 426 Squadron consisted of six North Star Aircrafts, and was later increased to twelve.

On August 7 as the Korean crisis deepened, the Canadian Government authorized the recruitment of the Canadian Army Special Force (CASF). These special forces included the second battalions of the Royal Canadian regiment (RCR); Princess Patricia's Canadian Light Infantry (PPCLI); the Royal 22nd Regiment (R 22 R); "C" Squadron of Lord Strathcona's Horse (Royal Canadian); 2nd Field Regiment Royal Canadian Horse Artillery (RCHA); 57th Canadian Independent Field Squadron; Royal Canadian Engineers (RCE); 25th Canadian Infantry Brigade Signal Squadron; Number 54 Canadian Transport Company; Royal Canadian Army Services Corps (RCASC); and

No. 25 Field Ambulance, Royal Canadian Army Medical Corps (RCAMC).

In February 1951, Canadian soldiers went into action in Korea, and on February 22, suffered their first casualties. Canadians, including Newfoundlanders, would spend three long years fighting in the hills, the swamps and rice paddies of Korea. Many of them during this period would pay the supreme sacrifice. Not only did our soldiers suffer casualties of the war, but while on the East Coast Patrol, the HMCS *Iroquois* received a direct hit from a shore battery. Three seamen were killed and ten were wounded,

On July 27, 1953, the Korean Armistice agreement was signed at Panmunjom, ending three years of fighting. Sixteen nations took part in the war of which 26,791 Canadian served, another 7,000 served in the theatre between the cease fire and 1955. During the war there were 1,558 fatal and non fatal Canadian Casualties. The names of the 516 Canadian War dead are recorded. There are 2,267 Servicemen buried in the United Nations Cemetery in Pusan, Korea. Of these 1,588 are Commonwealth soldiers including 378 Canadians. Sixteen Canadians are listed on the plaque, as well as those from Commonwealth Countries. A memorial to those whose burial places are unknown reads, "They died with men of other countries fighting to uphold the ideals of the United Nations."

# CANADA'S PARTICIPATION IN THE KOREAN WAR 1950-1953

## ROYAL CANADIAN NAVY (RCN)
HMCS *Athabaskan*
HMCS *Cayuga*
HMCS *Sioux*
HMCS *Nootka*
HMCS *Huron*
HMCS *Iroquois*
HMCS *Crusader*
HMCS *Haida*

## CANADIAN ARMY
Lord Strathcona's Horse (Royal Canadians)
2nd Field Regiment, Royal Canadian Horse Artillery, (RCHA)
1st Regiment, Royal Canadian Horse Artillery (RCHA)
81st Field Regiment, Royal Canadian Artillery (RCA)
The Corps of Royal Canadian Engineers (RCE)
The Royal Canadian Corps of Signals
The Royal Canadian Regiment (RCR), 1st Battalion, 2nd Battalion, 3rd Battalion
Princess Patricia's Canadian Light Infantry, 1st, 2nd and 3rd Battalion
Royal 22nd Regiment, 1st, 2nd and 3rd Battalion
The Royal Canadian Army Services Corps
The Royal Canadian Army Medical Corps
The Royal Canadian Dental Corps
Royal Canadian Ordnance Corps
The Corps of Royal Canadian Electrical and Mechanical Engineers
Royal Canadian Army Pay Corps
Royal Canadian Army Postal Corps
Royal Canadian Army Chaplain Corps
The Canadian Provost Corps
Canadian Intelligence Corps

## ROYAL CANADIAN AIR FORCE (RCAF)
No. 26 (Thunderbird) Squadron
(in addition, 22 RCAF pilots flew with the U.S. Fifth Air Force)

Donald Penney
St. Anthony
Royal Canadian Regiment
Killed in Action
July 20, 1953
One week before the war ended

The Grave of Donald Penney
United Nations Cemetery
Pusan, Korea

Hill 187 Korea, where Donald Penney was killed, July 20, 1953

### REMEMBERING HILL 187 IN KOREA
### FRANK SLADE

Hill 187 brings back memories to me as it was the last time I spent with my good buddy. Artillery fire lit up Hill 187 and it sounded like thunder from heaven. On Hill 187 two soldiers stood with 303 caliber rifles in their hands. They came from St. Anthony, a small town in Newfoundland.

We were in Dog Company, a Canadian Regiment who fought in three wars. This Regiment was called R.C.R. On the second day of May 1953, Dog Company was attacked by the North Korean Army and by the North Chinese. My buddy Don and I were on patrol with an old soldier, Sergeant McNeil who fought in Italy and Korea. We came across a mine field where fifteen Canadian soldiers lay dead.

After the raid was over and the morning shed its light, there were many dead and wounded and it wasn't a pretty sight. We spent another month on that old Hill 187, awake in fox-holes by day, sleeping in bunkers at night.

It was July 20, 1953, when 187 lit up. Mortar shell exploded all around Private Reid, my buddy and me. Then a shell exploded in our trench and it killed my buddy Don. Private Reid and I were okay. Sometimes when Don and I were alone on Hill 187, we would talk about our home St. Anthony. Our padre used to visit us every day. He would kneel with us and pray. Hill 187 is special to me. I think about it, I dream about it, what happened on it, and wish I could change it. That's all I can say.

This truck was on a mercy mission, taking several wounded soldiers to hospital in Korea, when it was hit by enemy fire killing the two officers in the front of the vehicle. The soldiers in the back escaped without injury, including Cpl. Frank Slade of St. Anthony.

Cpl. Frank Slade on the rifle range in Korea

Alexander Rowbottom                    Unidentified
Quirpon
Royal Canadian Regiment
Korean War
1950-1953
Killed in Action
October 23, 1952

Roy Wight
Shoal Brook, Bonne Bay
Korean War
1950-1953

Guns of the Royal Canadian Horse Artillery shelling enemy
positions at "Little Gibraltar" Korean Battlefields.

# A TEAR IN MY EYE

I was patrolling a compound when I heard a loud sound.
A shell had exploded, wounding a little Korean boy.
I ran to help him, he had lost two legs and one eye,
He was bleeding so badly, I thought he would die.

I picked him up gently, he was bleeding a lot,
I turned away my head, and wiped away a teardrop.
I spoke to him in English, but he didn't understand,
I couldn't speak his language, in that foreign land.

While I stood there waiting for the ambulance to appear,
I put up my hand, and wiped away another tear.
The medical team came, to take him away,
I'll always remember that terrible day.

When he got to the ambulance, he waved me good-bye,
I looked at him once more, and wiped a tear from my eye.
I tried to find out, if he lived or died,
No one could tell me, I had a tear in my eye.

Cruel men that cause wars, and little children to die,
They don't know how it feels, to have tears in their eyes.
When I'm all alone, and time passes by,
I still remember, that little Korean boy.


Frank Slade
Korean Veteran
St. Anthony

291

Frank Slade
St. Anthony
Royal Canadian Regiment
Paratrooper 27 jumps
Korea

Donald Moore
St. Anthony
Korea
1950-1953

Walter House
Bellburns
Korea
1950-1953

Sgt. John Bromley
Gray Island
C.M.C.G. Korea
1950-1953

Troops of the Royal Canadian Regiment and tanks of
Lord Strathcona's Horse,
Battlefields of Korea

L/S, Cpl. John Bromley
Grey Islands/S.E. Crouse
Royal Navy
World War II
Korea
1950-53

William Kenney
Conche
Korea
1950-53

After mastering the Russian language, Kenney was appointed Canadian Military Attachee, Moscow, USSR.

Prison of War Camp, Pusan, Korea
"A horrible place — a dump — everything stinks"

Village Residents celebrating Armistice Day
Tokchong, Korea, July 27, 1953

"Land of the Morning Calm", Korea

Tanks moving south, from the 38th Parallel, Korea

A Canadian Soldier kneels at the grave of a fallen comrade in the United Nations Cemetery, Pusan, Korea, April 1951

# Gulf War
## 1990-1991

# CANADIAN FORCES
# IN THE PERSIAN GULF

## 'OPERATION FRICTION'

On August 2, 1990, Iraq invaded Kuwait. The United Nations Security Council reacted swiftly on the same day with the adoption of Resolution 660, condemning the Iraqi invasion and demanding that Iraq withdraw immediately. This was the first of twelve resolutions which would culminate nearly four months later with Resolution 678, authorizing member states to use all necessary means to uphold Resolution 660.

Four days after the invasion, the United Nations passed Resolution 661, which called upon all states to impose strict economic sanctions on Iraq until it complied with Resolution 660. Many nations offered military forces to assist in this effort and, on August 10, the Prime Minister announced that Canada would contribute two destroyers and a supply ship to support a multinational effort in the Gulf region.

Over the next two weeks the destroyers HMCS *Athabaskan* and HMCS *Terra Nova*, and the supply ship HMCS *Protecteur* were extensively refitted and upgraded to permit them to participate in the interdiction mission outlined by the UN Security Council. Halifax Dockyard personnel worked long hours to install modern detection and weapons systems on board, while the Sea King helicopters carried by HMCS *Athabaskan* and HMCS *Protecteur* were equipped with a variety of defensive equipment and the Forward Looking Infrared (FLIR) system. Members of the Royal Canadian Artillery, equipped with Blowpipe and Javelin anti-aircraft missiles, also joined the ships.

On August 25, the United Nations Security Council adopted Resolution 665. It called upon participating nations to use necessary measures to halt all inward and outward maritime shipping to ensure compliance with Resolution 661.

A Canadian joint air and naval headquarters, under the command of Commodore Summers, was organized in October to command Canadian Forces units in-theatre and to coordinate all the carrier support activities involved in the effort. Canadian

Forces Middle East (CANFORME) Headquarters and Signals Squadron was established to provided communications within the operational theatre and with Canada.

Some of the forty-two Canadian Air Force personnel normally assigned to 552 AWACS (Airborne Warning and Control System) Wing at Tinker Air Force Base Oklahoma were deployed to the Gulf with their American crewmates. They were air defence operators and pilots who helped staff AWACS aircraft flying from bases in Saudi Arabia and monitoring air activity throughout the area. In addition, Canadian Air Force personnel assigned to NATO Airborne Early Warning Force at Geilenkirchen, Germany, were deployed to Konya, Turkey, with their NATO crews. This force, also flying AWACS aircraft, monitored air traffic in the northern Iraqi region. Normally 120 Canadians are stationed at Geilenkirchen, including pilots, air navigators, air weapons controllers, air defence technicians, radar technicians and communication operators.

In mid-December, 409 Squadron was replaced by 439 Tactical Fighter Squadron, also from Baden-Soellingen, and commanded by Lieutenant-Colonel Don Matthew. In addition, responsibility for the security of Canada Dry was transferred to Charlie Company, 1st Battalion, Royal 22e Regiment, which arrived from Canadian Force Base, Lahr, Germany.

On January 11, 1991, six more CF-18s from 416 Tactical Fighter Squadron, located at Canadian Forces Base Cold Lake, Alberta, were deployed to Qatar. This brought the total number of operational aircraft to twenty-four. At the same time, a Canadian Forces Boeing 707 was deployed to Qatar to assist in refueling Canadian and other allied aircraft.

On New Year's Day, 1991, a replacement crew for HMCS *Protecteur* left Halifax by air to take over duties in the Gulf. Three days later, HMCS *Huron* sailed from British Columbia for Halifax to undergo refit before sailing for the Gulf.

# OPERATION DESERT STORM – THE AIR WAR

In November, the United Nations passed Resolution 678, which set January 15, 1991, as the deadline for Iraq's unconditional withdrawal from Kuwait. The resolution also authorized United Nations member states to use all necessary means to uphold and implement Resolution 660 and subsequent applicable resolutions.

As the deadline drew closer, last minute negotiations failed. At 3 a.m. on January 17 (Gulf time), less than twenty-four hours after the UN deadline passed, Operation Desert Storm began with air strikes against military targets in Iraq and Kuwait.

When hostilities broke out, Captain Duncan ('Dusty') Miller ordered the Canadian Naval Task Group to the southern Gulf area and assumed command of the newly formed Combat Logistics Force – a multinational force of about twenty-four ships from various UN countries. HMCS *Protecteur* joined other supply ships while HMCS *Terra Nova* and HMCS *Athabaskan* assumed responsibility for defensive escort of the force. Captain (N) Miller was responsible for escorting and protecting allied supply ships and scheduling all logistic resupply on behalf of the battle force commander.

Under his direction, tankers and supply ships carrying food, ammunition, fuel, spare parts, stores and provisions were escorted north to rendezvous points, where they resupplied warships operating near Iraq and Kuwait's.

On the same day that Operation Desert Storm began, it was announced that one Canadian Field Hospital would move from Petawawa, Ontario, to Saudi Arabia in response to a request from British authorities for augmentation of medical treatment resources. A staff of 550 deployed to the Gulf in late January. The hospital flew the Canadian flag and was commanded by the commander of the Canadian Forces Middle East, while tactical control was delegated to the commander of the British forces.

The hospital was initially deployed to Al Jubayl, Saudi Arabia, and later moved closer to within forty kilometres of the front. During this time, the staff endured the harsh climate of the Saudi desert. Temperatures regularly rose to the mid-thirties during the day and fell to below freezing at night. Sandstorms were frequent. Once the oil fields were set alight in Kuwait, the staff witnessed massive clouds filled with dark oil particles. The clouds literally made day as dark as night, and throughout the region, the rain was heavy and oily. The hospital provided medical treatment for British combat casualties and Iraqi prisoners of war during Desert Storm.

Until this point, the primary role of Canada's fighter aircraft was Combat Air Patrol in the central Gulf, providing air cover for the Canadian Naval Task Group. On January 17, the Chief of the Defence Staff announced that the fighters' role has been expanded to include sweep and escort duties in support of other elements of allied air forces. Canadian pilots carried out this first sweep and escort mission over enemy territory in late January.

On February 20, an air-to-ground attack role was authorized for Canadian CF-18s. Combat Air Patrols to protect allied shipping continued.

## THE GROUND WAR

On the night of February 23, the long awaited allied ground offensive began. The ground forces moved quickly, sustaining extremely light casualties. Thousands of Iraqi soldiers surrendered and were made prisoners of war.

On the night of February 27 – 100 hours after the beginning of the ground war and six weeks from the beginning of Operation Desert Storm – coalition forces suspended offensive combat operations. The allies set certain terms for Iraq to meet and a formal cease fire was ratified.

With the end of the war, the scheduled deployments of HMCS *Restigouche* and HMCS *Provider* were cancelled on March 1. They had been scheduled to replace ships which had sailed for the Gulf the previous week.

In mid-March, twenty-three Canadian Forces personnel already in the theatre formed a Military Engineer Explosive Ordnance Disposal Troop which became part of a multinational munitions clearance organization. The Canadian team assisted in the clearing of explosive materials out of Kuwait City.

The first Canadian personnel began arriving home from the Gulf in early March. Virtually all Canadian personnel, except the crew of HMCS *Huron*, had returned to their bases in Canada and Germany by mid-April. HMCS *Huron*, which joined the multinational forces in the Gulf near the end of April, was scheduled to depart the Persian Gulf at the end of June and was expected to arrive home in Esquimalt, B.C., in early August. The cease-fire with Iraq was formally ratified in early April.

A Kurdish rebellion developed in northern Iraq in the aftermath of the Gulf War. When the rebellion was over, thousands of Kurdish refugees began streaming across the border into southern Turkey and Iran. The Canadian Forces provided Hercules aircraft and a Boeing 707 to carry relief supplies into the area. On April 12, it was announced that elements of 4 Field Ambulance, comprised of sixty personnel and their equipment, would deploy from Germany to southern Turkey to provide medical aid to the refugees.

Four days later, the Department of National Defence and the Department of External Affairs announced that Canada would participate in the United Nations Iraq/Kuwait Observer Mission (UNIKOM). The Canadian Forces had provided a senior officer to serve as Deputy Chief of Staff Operations with UNIKOM and a contingent of approximately 300 engineers. The contingent was deployed in May to a demilitarized zone along the Iraq/Kuwait border.

The UNIKOM force was the first in the United Nations history to include personnel from all five permanent members of the United Nations Security Council. Their job was to ensure there were no military personnel or installations belonging to either country in the zone. Canadian Forces engineers were involved in making the demilitarized zone safe from unexploded mines or bombs.

## IN SUMMARY

From the beginning of their deployment until the end of hostilities, the ships of the Canadian Naval Task Group steamed more than 98,000 nautical miles. The Sea King helicopters flew more than 2,000 hours. The Task Group carried out 1,877 of 7,645

(24.6 percent) interception of hailings of suspect vessels during the interdiction effort.

Thirty-four CF-18 fighter jets were deployed to the Gulf, with a maximum of twenty-six in-theatre at any one time, plus one Boeing 707 refueller and a Challenger liaison aircraft. The CF-18s flew 5,730 hours, the Boeing, 306 hours and the Challenger, 170 hours.

Air Transport Group ferried more than 2.5 million kilograms of cargo to the Gulf. More than ninety thousand kilograms of mail were sent to or from Canadians in the Gulf.

An estimated 4,000 Canadian Forces personnel served in-theatre between August 1990 and April 1991 with a maximum of 2,500 in-theatre at any one time. Approximately 2,000 more in Germany and Canada were involved in direct support of the war effort.

Canadians sustained no operational casualties during the course of the war.

In the Persian Gulf, 1991

Left to Right: L/S Glen Colbourne, O/S Lorne Slade and M/S
Jerry Colbourne

HMCS *Protecteur*
Gulf War, 1991

Sheila Keats-Robertson
St. Anthony
Royal Canadian Navy
Gulf War 1991

Bruce Hall
Daniel's Harbour
Royal Canadian Navy
Gulf War 1991

Lorne Slade
St. Anthony
Royal Canadian Navy
Gulf War 1991

Rene McDonald
Goose Bay
Royal Canadian Navy
Gulf War 1991

HMCS *Athabaskan*
Gulf War 1991

LS Glen Colbourne CD
St. Anthony
Gulf War 1991

Benson Cull
St. Anthony
Gulf War 1991

Glen Colbourne
In Action Dress
Gulf War 1991

PO1 Jerry Colbourne
St. Anthony
Gulf War 1991

HMCS *Terra Nova*
Gulf War 1991

# REMEMBRANCE DAY
## THE CALL
### Peter C. Mars

I hold this emblem of dead youth, clasped tightly to my breast,
As I held you when a baby sweet, and lulled you to your rest;
The scarlet of the poppies blooms, like babies lips are red,
And I croon o'er them the lullabys I sang beside your bed.

Few were the years I held you, but life seemed full to me;
I dreamed my thoughts of greatness for the man my boy would be,
I treasured you and loved you because you were my own;
But now you sleep in Flanders Field and I am all alone.

Alone with memories only of the boy who went away,
The gallant lad who kissed me with a laugh so light and gay
I hear again your laughter and I see your good-bye smile;
For the poppy brings its message, and I wait a little while.

Each year the poppy blossoms, and sheds its scarlet flowers
O'er graves where heroes sleep and rest, who live a few brief hours;
And there my boy is resting, 'mongst gallant men and brave;
And though my heart is breaking, yet I'm glad "he died to save."

Each year the Poppy brings to me its message so sweet,
The time is passing quickly 'till we again will meet;
I would not have it otherwise, although I gave "my all,"
And I'm glad God gave me the courage when my baby heard
"The Call."

# VETERAN URGES EVERYONE TO PAY TRIBUTE TO THOSE WHO DIED

## EDITOR, THE MORNING SUN:

Remembrance Day, November 11: Each year the ranks grow thinner, the steps are slower. It's obvious that time is taking its toll on the ageing but stalwart who come out to mark this day of solemnity and quiet reflections; and pay tribute to their Brothers and Sisters who paid the Supreme Sacrifice, many of them resting in the bloody battlefields upon which they fought.

Those of us who went overseas in World War II will recall the Dark Days of 1940-1941 when Britain and the Commonwealth stood alone against the all-powerful Nazi Juggernaut. We will remember those brave pilots and air crews who lost their lives in the Battle of Britain, and the Naval and Merchant Seamen who met a Watery Grave in their struggle for survival against the U-boats known as "The Wolf Packs" in the Battle of the North Atlantic. Let us remember the courageous soldiers who fought and died in Hong Kong, Burma, and the Southeast Asia approaches, and the Hell holes of North Africa and the European continent. The survivors will be offering a silent prayer. Veterans of the Korean Conflict, the unknown war, will reflect on their seemingly futile struggle against a strange enemy in a strange land. Let's hope their comrades, left behind, did not die in vain.

Even today, when the world should be at peace, Canadian men and women in our Armed Forces are risking their lives in trouble spots around the world; some have died in the line of duty. We must not forget their sacrifice in the cause of peace. So, on this Remembrance Day, November 11, let us bow our heads for a brief moment in silent tribute to those who gave their lives in the cause of freedom and made it possible for us to enjoy the privileges and benefits bestowed on people all over the world.

John Bromley, CD
Grey Islands
Parkville, B.C.

# THE FOLLOWING IS A LIST OF VETERANS OF THE NORTH WHO SERVED THEIR COUNTRY IN WAR, BUT WHOSE PICTURES DO NOT APPEAR IN THIS BOOK

## ROYAL NEWFOUNDLAND REGIMENT, WORLD WAR I

| | | |
|---|---|---|
| Alcock, Harvey | Griquet | |
| Ash, Albert | Labrador | |
| Bird, Silas | Cartwright | |
| Bradbury, George | Labrador | |
| Bright, Peter | Labrador | |
| Broomfield, James | Labrador | |
| Broomfield, Wilfred | Labrador | |
| Brown, Robert | Labrador | |
| Budden, Selby | Jackson's Arm | |
| Budgell, Stanley | St. Anthony | |
| Caines, Garfield | Bonne Bay | |
| Caines, Isaac | Port Saunders | |
| Caines, Walter | Port Saunders | |
| Canning, Ambrose | Labrador | |
| Caravan, Nathaniel | Bonne Bay | |
| Cassell, Dadarias | Whooping Harbour | |
| Chaytor, James | Grey Islands | |
| Compton, Charles | Griquet ? | |
| Compton, Walter | Jackson's Arm | |
| Coombs, George | Labrador | |
| Critch, Jesse | Norris Point | |
| Critch, William | St. Anthony | |
| Crocker, Andrew | Trout River | |
| Crocker, Bryant | Trout River | |
| Davis, Charles | Labrador | |
| Dean, Henry | St. Anthony | |
| Diamond, Objiah | Flowers Cove | |
| Diamond, Joseph | Flowers Cove | |
| Dunn, Isaac | Labrador | |
| Ellis, Abram | Port Saunders | Killed in Action, April 13, 1918 |
| Ellsworth, Andrew | Rocky Harbour | |
| Ellsworth, John | Rocky Harbour | |
| Fields, Charles | Cooks Harbour | Killed in Action, October 9, 1917 |
| Flag, Jonathan | Labrador | |
| Flowers, Thomas | Labrador | |
| Ford, Fred | Nain | |
| Ford, James | Nain | Died February 26, 1916 |
| Ford, Simeon | Jackson's Arm | |
| Ford, Thomas | Jackson's Arm | Died of Wounds, May 25, 1917 |

| | | |
|---|---|---|
| Gilley, Job | Bonne Bay | |
| Goudie, James | Labrador | |
| Groves, Daniel L/C | Goose Bay | |
| Halfyard, John | Bonne Bay | Died of Wounds, October 21, 1918 |
| Halfyard, Wallace | Bonne Bay | Killed in Action, May, 25, 1918 |
| Hann, Bregam | Bonne Bay | Died of Wounds, September 30, 1918 |
| Harding, George | Bonne Bay | |
| House, Jacob | Bellburns | |
| Hull, Harvey L/C | Seal Island | |
| Hutchings, William | Bonne Bay | Presumed Dead, April 13, 1918 |
| James, Fraser Wilson | Western Arm | |
| Janes, Peter | Grey Island | |
| Kennedy, James | Brig Bay | |
| Keough, Michael | Bonne Bay | |
| Keppenhook, John | Labrador | |
| Knott, William | Sally's Cove | Died of Wounds, November 21, 1917 |
| Lane, Job | Labrador | |
| Learning, Francis | Labrador | |
| Lewis, Robert | Port Saunders | |
| Lloyd, Robert | Labrador | |
| McKenzie, William | Labrador | Killed in Action, November 20, 1917 |
| McLean, Murdock | Labrador | |
| Major, John T. | Norris Point | Died June 7, 1918 |
| Martin, Nathaniel | Bonne Bay | |
| Matthews, Fred | St. Anthony | |
| Mesher, Charles | Rigolet | Presumed Dead, November 17, 1917 |
| Michelin, Charles | North West River, Labrador | |
| Michelin, Joseph | North West River, Labrador | |
| Michelin, Robert | North West River, Labrador | |
| Moores, Jonathan | Woody Point | |
| Nicholas, John | Harbour Deep | |
| Oates, Abner | Norris Point | |
| Offery, Joseph | Port au Choix | |
| Pardy, Austin | Cartwright | |
| Parsons, Taylor | Trout River | |
| Parsons, William | Bonne Bay | |
| Patey, Fredrick | St. Anthony | |
| Patey, Gilbert | Big Brehat | |
| Patey, Henry | Port Saunders | |
| Patey, John | St. Lunaire | |
| Payne, John | Bonne Bay | |
| Payne, Leslie | Bonne Bay | |
| Payne, Norman | Parsons Pond | Killed in Action, April 13, 1918 |
| Payne, Wilson | Bonne Bay | |
| Perry, Reuben | River of Ponds | |
| Pynn, Charles | Quirpon | |

| | | |
|---|---|---|
| Pittman, Manuel | Conche | |
| Pollard, William | Harbour Deep | Killed in Action, April 13, 1918 |
| Prosper, Hayward | Woody Point | |
| Prosper, John | Woody Point | |
| Randell, Thomas | Little Harbour Deep | |
| Randell, William | Cooney Arm | |
| Reid, Arthur | Bonne Bay | |
| Reid, Chesley | Jackson's Arm | |
| Roberts, Rendell | Bonne Bay | |
| Rumbolt, Ezekiah | Norris Point | |
| Rumbolt, Lemiel | Bonne Bay | |
| Saunders, Fredrick | Griquet | Presumed Dead, May 9, 1917 |
| Seaward, Edward | Bonne Bay | |
| Skanes, Charles | Cow Head | |
| Smith, Edward | Labrador | Died October 14, 1918 |
| Smith, Fredrick | Griquet | |
| Steven, James | Labrador | |
| Stickland, Ephriam | Bonne Bay | |
| Thatchell, Henry | Bartlett's Harbour | |
| Tomisheny, George | Labrador | Killed in Action, October 3, 1918 |
| Tucker, George | Port Saunders | |
| Welsh, Richard | Bonne Bay | |
| White, Rennie | Englee | |
| Winters, William | Labrador | |

## ROYAL NAVAL RESERVE, WORLD WAR I

| | |
|---|---|
| Baines, Michael | Shoal Cove West |
| Bussey, Jacob | St. Lunaire |
| Bussey, Thomas | St. Lunaire |
| Butt, John C. | Rocky Harbour |
| Butt, Peter | Rocky Harbour |
| Chambers, John | Flower's Cove |
| Coates, George | Eddies Cove East |
| Coles, Elias | Squid Cove |
| Coles, Pius | Port Saunders |
| Coles, William A. | Sandy Cove |
| Coles, William J. | Port Saunders |
| Compton, John | Englee |
| Crocker, Job | Trout River |
| Crocker, Wallace J. | Trout River |
| Currel, John | Labrador |
| Diamond, Absolom | Flower's Cove |
| Duncan, John | Flower's Cove |

| | |
|---|---|
| Ford, S. | Jackson's Arm |
| Galliott, William | Straits |
| Gaulton, Reuben | Flower's Cove |
| Genge, Henry | Flower's Cove |
| Genge, Jacob | Flower's Cove |
| Genge, Lambert | Flower's Cove |
| Gibbons, Isaac | Current Island |
| Gillam, William J. | Bonne Bay |
| Gould, Elijah | River of Ponds |
| Halfyard, Alfred | Bonne Bay |
| Halfyard, George | Bonne Bay |
| Hillier, Albert M. | Griquet |
| Hiscock, William | Norris Point |
| Holwell, James | Labrador |
| Lawless, Leo | Flower's Cove |
| Lawless, Mark | Flower's Cove |
| Loder, Allan | Griquet |
| Noel, George E. | Bonne Bay |
| Parsons, Samuel F. | Bonne Bay |
| Parsons, William | Port au Choix |
| Patey, Leonard | Port Saunders |
| Payne, Gordon | Daniel's Harbour |
| Pittman, Benjamin | Bonne Bay |
| Pittman, Silas | Bonne Bay |
| Plowman, Edward | Port Saunders |
| Prosper, William | Bonne Bay |
| Pynn, Albert | Quirpon |
| Pynn, Fredrick | Quirpon |
| Rose, Arthur | Flower's Cove |
| Smith, Arthur | Griquet |
| Tucker, Phillip | Rocky Harbour |
| Walsh, Douglas | Bellburns |
| Walsh, Patrick | Flower's Cove |
| Walsh, Patrick S. | Flower's Cove |
| Way, Daniel F. | Savage Cove |
| Way, Stephen | Savage Cove |
| Whalen, Caleb | Flower's Cove |
| Whalen, John S. | Flower's Cove |
| Whalen, Stephen | Flower's Cove |
| Young, George | Parson's Pond |

## ROYAL NAVY, WORLD WAR II

| | |
|---|---|
| Boyd, Augustus | Bonne Bay |
| Brown, Charles H. | Rocky Harbour |

| | |
|---|---|
| Butt, Garland | Lomond |
| Butt, George W. | Rocky Harbour |
| Crocker, Selby | Trout River |
| Cullihall, Gordon | Rocky Harbour |
| Decker, Maxwell | Cape Onion |
| Eisan, Reginald | Port Saunders |
| Gould, Joseph | Port Saunders |
| Guy, Garland | Bonne Bay |
| Hefler, Francis | Cartwright |
| Hewlin, Liewellyn | Spirity Cove |
| Hoddinott, Gordon | Brig Bay |
| Hutchings, Rufus | Cow Head |
| Jennix, John | Port au Choix |
| Martin, George | Cartwright |
| Martin, Howard | Cartwright |
| Noel, Thomas J. | Woody Point |
| Noel, William | Woody Point |
| Parsons, Norman | Rocky Harbour |
| Pike, Charles | Port Saunders |
| Pike, Harley | Port Saunders |
| Pike, Joseph | Port Saunders |
| Rumbolt, Austin | Port au Choix |
| Rumbolt, Jerome | Port au Choix |
| Shears, Roland | Woody Point |
| Smart, Wilson | Indian Cove, Labrador |
| Snow, Charles | Norris Point |
| Sutton, Richard | Lanse Au Loop |
| Symmonds, Garfield | Bonne Bay |
| Warren, Phillip | Flower's Cove |
| Way, Moses | Savage Cove |
| Webb, Edward | Hopedale |
| Whalen, Eric | Flower's Cove |
| Wight, Victor | Bonne Bay |
| Willette, John | Bonne Bay |

Note: Some of the unidentified veterans in this book may be included in these lists.

The addresses given are those listed in the official listings of veterans. Listings for others such as Air Force, 166th, 59th Regiments, Forestry, Merchant Navy, Korean and Gulf were not available to the author.

There are probably other veterans from the Northern Peninsula and Labrado, whose names do not appear on this list as they were not available to the author.

# EPILOGUE

As we turn the final pages of this book, dedicated to the lives of some of the bravest people ever to walk on this planet, some may ask, "Was the price paid for freedom too high?" Any life lost, bodies wrecked, or minds destroyed is a very high price to pay.

Then we stop, we ask ourselves, "Was there another way?" Probably if it were today things could be somewhat different, with today's modern inventions in warfare technology. But regardless of the war material used, the loss of lives and sufferings of wars still remain, and one thing which never changes, is the suffering brought about as a result of war.

This book is a story in pictures and words of those from the Great Northern Peninsula and Labrador who sacrificed much that we may have the freedom we enjoy today. We also dedicate this book to those who do not appear, but whose contributions to the peace we enjoy today is of the same equality. Many of these lie in marked and unmarked graves in foreign soil, others in the sea; for some their spirits lie in empty graves back home as a constant reminder of the terrible price paid for peace in our land.

For those who came back, many show the physical scars as well as the mental sufferings. After most of them have departed, we will ask, "Were our veterans treated fairly after war, in recognition for their contribution to peace in our land?" There are many who share the view that we should have done more; others would say what we gave them was far too late in coming, almost too late for many of them to enjoy.

I am sure I share the prayers, wishes and hopes of all people, that after all of our present veterans have gone to their just reward, there will be no more War Veterans. One may ask, "How can we have a world with no War Veterans?" The answer, a world with no wars, how beautiful it would be if down the road of time, we would be able to say, "Imagine all the money which could be channeled into the starving people of the world, and locally into our health care system here at home." Wishful thinking, maybe, but still a wish.

# NAJISIUK

Tatsuma atuagaup paginangit nunguvalliatillugit, ilingattitaujuit ilanginnut pilluangusimajunut tumani nunatsuami pisusimajut ubvalu asiani nunami.

Ilangit apitsuKattavut, Akilittausimavan silakKijanitsak akitujosimamman? Inosingit asiusimajuit, timingit siKuttitausimajut ubvalu isumangit piugilititausimajut akitujuvatsuanguvut akiligasuagiangit.

NukKkaKattavugut, imminik apigidluta, Asiagut pigunnasimavan? ImmaKa ullumiuppat sunait adjiungitogajakKut, ullumi inogusiulittut nutangulimmata ilingajuit unatannimut. Unatattunut ilingajunik pitaKagaluappat atuttauKattajunik, inoset asiusimajut ammalu siunniusimajut unatannisuami suli taimailingavut, ammmalu atautsik asiangugunnangituk, ommatet annisimajut ammalu siuniusimajut tamanna pitjutauva unatannimon.

Tanna atuagak allatausimavuk adjinguaKatillugu uKausigisimajangit Great Northern Peninsula-mit Labrador-imilly, inosingit uKumaittukosimajut ullumi uvagut silakKijakKudluta. Ammalu tanna atuagak iligattijavut taikkununga tamani allatausimagitunt, tavatuk ikajugnnasimajuit silakKijagiamut ullumi adjigetitauvuk. Unuttuit iluviKavuty nalunaikkutalet nalunaikkutaKangituillu nunami ilitannangitumi. Asingit imappimejut, ilanginnut inosingi???iluvinejut sunaugatik angiggamini ikKaigutauKattadlutik kappianattusuamik akilittaugialimmik silkKijagiamut nunattini.

Taikkua utisimajuit, takutitsiKattavut kenangit Kiligulet ammalu isumangit piujogunnaitut. Illonangit aullasimalittilugit, apigiKattavugut, Unatattivinivut adjigetsiajumik pijauKattavan, unatannisuamekKatillugit kiggatudlutik silakKigjanitsatinik nunattini. Unuttuit uKalaKattavut takunnausiminik uvagut anginitsamik pisimajutsauvugut, asivut uKaKattavut, aittusimajavut upaludluta, upalukasammagidluta unuttuit silakKijanitsanginnut.

Kaujimavunga tutsiadlutik KinugaKattajut ammalu Kanuttoningit ilonnatik inuit, ullumiujuk Unatattivut aittutausimalippata akiliusiaminik, UnatattiviniKalagunnaiKuk.

ApitsujuKagajakKuk, Kanuk nunatsuaKagajakKita UnatattiviniKagata? Kiujavuk, nunatsuami unatanniKangipat, PiujummagiugajakKuk Kangatuinnak sivunitsatinni, uKasonguligutta, unatanniKagunnaitumik, pinniagutingit nanitu-innak nunatsuami. Isumagilautsigik kenaujaluvinet aulataugajat-tut aititauKattalutik pillilittunut inunnut nunatsuami, nunattinilu sukatailigiamut iligattilugit tamani angiggatinni, isumajannikut Kanuttoniujuk, immaKa, suli Kanuttojut.

Allasimajuk

# INDEX OF PHOTOGRAPHS

Alcock, Augustus 56
Allangham, John 125
Allangham, William 125
Allingham, David 208
Andrews, Archabold 204
Andrews, Archabold 266
Andrews, Herbert 194
Andrews, Herbert 204
Ash, Archabold 43

Barney, John Charles 115
Barney, William H. 115
Barrett, Clemence 224
Battle of Bazentin  50
Battle of Gallipoli, Soldier
Helps His Comrade 14
Beaufield, Horace 198
Beaufield, Malcholm 127
Beaumont Hamel,
Attacking Troops 47
Beaumont Hamel,
Bombardment 39
Beaumont Hamel, Bronze
Plaques 31
Beaumont Hamel, Caribou
Memorial 33
Beaumont Hamel, Charred
Battlefields 25
Beaumont Hamel, Danger
Tree 29
Beaumont Hamel, General
View of Battlefield 30
Beaumont Hamel, Going
Over the Top 20
Beaumont Hamel, Graves
34
Beaumont Hamel, St.
John's Road  23
Beaumont Hamel,
Stretcher-bearers 37
Beaumont Hamel, Wounded
Soldiers 48
Bessey, Reuben 92
Bessey, Reuben 127
Bessey, William H. 197
Biggin, Cornelious 181
Biggin, Leonard 184
Biles, Daniel 96
Biles, Wesley 197
*Bismark* 179
Boyd, Arthur 251
Boyd, Joseph F. 84
Bradley, Harry 178

Breen, Michael 269
Brett, Douglas 199
Brett, Douglas 204
Bromley, John 292
Bromley, John 294
Bromley, John A. 187
Brown, Abraham 201
Brown, Hrebert S. 156
Brown, Robert 118
Bulger, David 98
Bussey, Garland 120
Bussey, Samuel 126
Byrne, Michael 261

Canning, Rene 176
Carpenter, James Ronald
162
Carroll, Bernard M. 54
Casey, Bernard 200
Cassino, Italy - 166th
Regiment  228
Cassino, Italy - 166th
Regiment  230
Chambers, Abraham 272
Chambers, Absalom 203
Chambers, Absolom 78
Chambers, Absolom 176
Chambers, George 176
Chambers, George 203
Chambers, George 208
Chambers, Cyril 265
Chambers, Ronald 203
Clark, William 106
Coates, Phillip 123
Colbourne, Absolom 169
Colbourne, Garland 270
Colbourne, Glen 306
Colbourne, Glen 309
Colbourne, Jerry 306
Colbourne, Jerry 309
Coles, Albert V. 40
Coles, George 128
Compass Rose Memorial
275
Cull, Benson 309
Cull, Fremontia Augustus
184

Decker, Edgar 178
Decker, Haylock 180
Dempster, Richard 116
Diamond, Wilson Woodrow
159

Dinney, Elias 93
Dinney, George 93
Dinney, Roland 93
Dobbin, Brendon B. 196
Doyle, Henry 262
Doyle, James 262
Dumaresque, John   173
Dumaresque, John Anley
250
Dumphy, Thomas 189

Elgar, Charles John 105
Elliott, Alpheus 84
Elliott, Alpheus 102
Elliott, Erastus 103
Elliott, Leonard 190
Elliott, Thomas 118
Elliott, William 142
Elson, Albert 95
Elson, Albert 106

Fennimore, Ben 265
Fennimore, William F. 91
Fennimore, William G. 154
Fillier, Albert 89
Fitzgerald, Ronald 252
Fitzpatrick, Alphonsus 46
Fitzpatrick, Leo Joe 76
Fitzpatrick, Leo Joseph 83
Fogarty, Joseph 180
Fogarty, Patrick 180
Foley, Ted 123
Freda, Frederick 36

Galliott, Henry 176
Galliott, Henry W.   181
Genge, Caleb 268
Genge, Henry 128
Genge, Pius 208
Gibbons, Abe 207
Gibbons, Abraham 224
Gibbons, John 118
Gill, Arthur F. 59
Gillard, C.L. (Lea) 174
Gould, Andrew 198
Gould, Andrew 207
Gould, George 268
Government Telegram 157
Green, Edward James 104
Green, Freeman 201
Guinchard, Cornelious 182

Halifax Bomber, WWII 249

Hall, Bruce 307
Hancock, Albert 64
Hancock, Charles N. 166
Hancock, Simon 264
Hancock, Simon Raymond 260
Hann, Charles 66
Hann, Robert 65
Hatcher, Samuel 240
Hedderson, Edgar 182
Hedderson, Heber 182
Hill, Arthur 140
Hill, Jacob 140
Hillier, Archabold 126
Hillier, Donald 172
Hillier, Francis 172
Hinks, Arthur 263
HMCS *Athabaskan* 308
HMCS *Protecteur* 306
HMCS *Terra Nova* 310
HMCS *Valleyfield* 167
HMS *Ark Royal* 175
HMS *Avenger* 153
HMS *Fiji* 206
HMS *Hood* 183
HMS *Liverpool* 186
HMS *Newmarket* 164
HMS *Revenge* 171
HMS *Rodney* 191
HMS *Rodney* 193
HMS *Stanley* 155
HMS Trawler *Loch Maree* 140
HMS *Vervain* 161
HMS *Warspite* 131
Hoddinott, Howard Harvey 251
Hodge, George W. 124
Hodge, James 128
Hodge, John 271
Hodge, Samuel 270
Horrors of War, Limbless WWI Veterans 13
House, Arthur 100
House, Emmanuel 119
House, Gordon 192
House, Jesse 118
House, Luke 122
House, Walter 292
Hynes, Lawrence 120

James, John Anley 112
Johnson, Augustus 81
Johnson, Dudley 81
Johnson, Dudley 99
Just Nuisance 219

Keats-Robertson, Sheila 307
Kennedy, Stanley 185
Kenney, William 294
Korean War, Celebrating Armistice Day 296
Korean War, Hill 187 286
Korean War, Land of the Morning Calm 296
Korean War, Little Gibraltar 290
Korean War, Prisoner of War Camp 295
Korean War, Royal Canadian Regiment and Lord Strathcona's Horse 293
Korean War, Soldier Awaiting Medical Attention 280
Korean War, Tanks on 38th Parallel 297
Korean War, United Nations Cemetery 298
Korean War, Vehicle Bombing 287

Laing, Curling 253
Letto, Albert Peter 241
Letto, Emmanuel David 255
Lewis, George 86
Lewis, Leo 261
Loder, Frederick 99
Luther, John 180
Luther, John - Valentine 177

Manuel, Roland 119
Manuel, Theophilus 123
*Maravel* 215
Marshall, Jack 207
Martin, Frank 107
Martin, Robert James 107
Mazzagrognia, Italy 232
McDonald, George 248
McDonald, Rene 307
McLean, John 207
McLean, John 208
Mesher, Jonathan 120
Mine Sweeper, BYMS 807 169
Mitchelmore, Churchill 172
Mitchelmore, George 55
Mitchelmore, Isaac 55
Mitchelmore, Malcolm 266
Mitchelmore, Samuel 40

Moore, Donald 95
Moore, Donald 106
Moore, Donald 292
Moore, Fredrick 168
Moores, Jacob 82
Moores, Stephen 116

Mugford, Ambrose 119
Myers, Edward 264

Newman, Shem 269
Nicholas, Arthur 94
Noble, Wilfred J. 166
Normandy, 59th Heavy Regiment 244
Normandy, Howitzer, 59th Heavy Regiment 243
Normandy, Long Tom, 59th Heavy Regiment 243
Normore, Paula 115
Norris, Stephen 42
Noseworthy, Gilbert 173
Noseworthy, Lionel 201
Noseworthy, Nora 256

O'Neill, Patrick 189
Ollerhead, Roland 182
Osmond, Gordon 204

Pardy, Elmer C. 189
Pardy, Manuel 72
Pardy, Willis 189
Parsons, Stella 256
Patey, Donald 253
Patey, Donald 254
Patey, Fredrick 142
Patey, Herbert 88
Patey, Herbert 91
Patey, Herbert 106
Patey, Isaac 267
Patey, Noah 78
Patey, Norman Lance 239
Patey, Reuben 88
Patey, Reuben 94
Patey, Reuben 169
Patey, Richard 278
Patey, Stanley 192
Patey, William 120
Patey, William 123
Patey, William W. 51
Payne, Garland 139
Payne, James 121
Penney, Albert 121
Penney, Clem 88
Penney, Clem 90
Penney, Clem 106

Penney, Clemence 102
Penney, Donald 285
Penney, George 139
Penney, Harvey 202
Penney, Henry 87
Perry, Robert Solomon 199
Pilgrim, Allan 98
Pilgrim, Bickle R. 87
Pilgrim, Ernest 86
Pilgrim, Lewis 98
Pilgrim, Orland 81
Pilgrim, Sidney 97
Pittman, Abe 207
Pittman, Abe 208
Pittman, Chesley 207
Pittman, John 126
Pittman, John 207
Ploughman, William 263
Power, Daniel B. 181
Puddicombe, William 114
Pye, Hayward 76
Pye, Hayward 95
Pye, Walter 95
Pynn, Abil 190

Reardon, Anthony 192
Reardon, Anthony 204
Reardon, Herbert 227
Reardon, James 192
Reeves, Stanley 264
Reid, Levi 100
Reid, Levi F. 181
Richards, David 52
Richards, Joseph 165
Richards, Richard 277
Ricketts, Thomas 68
Ricketts, Thomas 70
Ricks, Simon 67
Roberts, Esau 141
Roberts, Hedley V. 141
Roberts, Thomas 90
Roberts, Roland 178
Roberts, Roland 266
Ropson, Frank 97
Rose, Albert S. 73
Rowbottom, Alexander 288
Rowbottom, Herbert 81
Rowsell, Donald 252
Royal Newfoundland
Regiment, No Smiles for the
Camera, WWI 12
Royal Newfoundland
Regiment, Preparing for
War, WWI 11

Sampson, Chesley 272

Sampson, Thomas Gardner
151
Sampson, William 207
Sampson, William 208
Sampson, William 272
Saunders, Charles 113
Saunders, John 113
Scanlon, Joseph 104
Shears, Walter 178
Sheppard, Carl 207
Sheppard, Herbert 195
Sheppard, Herbert 207
Shiwak, John 57
Shiwak, John 89
Simms, Alexander 199
Simms, Arthur 77
Simms, Beattie 88
Simms, Charles 277
Simms, Francis 174
Simms, George P. 38
Simms, Herbert 85
Simms, Herbert 106
Simms, Leaton 36
Simms, Leaton 60
Simms, Reuben 195
Simms, Richard 278
Simms, Robert 165
Simms, Roland 36
Slade, Frank 287
Slade, Frank 292
Slade, Lorne 306
Slade, Lorne 307
Slade, Solomon 86
Smith, John 122
Smith, Norman R. 163
Snook, Alfred 103
Snow, Ernest 86
Snow, Joseph 96
S.S. Corsican 117
Stone, Bede 172
Strangemore, Everton 205
Stickland, Meshach 82
Stickland, Peter 93
Sutton, William 264

Thomas, Gordon 216
Toope, Benjamin 270
Tracey, William 98
Troy, Leo 200
Tucker, Absolom 124
Tucker, Charles 202
Tucker, George 207
Tucker, George 208
Tucker, Henry 207
Tucker, Henry 208
Tucker, Roland 194

Tucker, Stephen 229
Tucker, Stephen 231
Tucker, Steve 208
Tucker, Thomas 92
Tucker, Thomas 127

Unidentified 106
Unidentified 130
Unidentified 132
Unidentified 133
Unidentified 134
Unidentified 135
Unidentified 136
Unidentified 137
Unidentified 138
Unidentified 176
Unidentified 254
Unidentified 267
Unidentified 288

Verge, Enos 121

Ward, Henry 105
Warford, James 85
Warren, Caleb 126
Way, Darius 266
Way, Henry T. 267
Way, Richard 267
Way, Stephen 271
Whalen, Edward 199
Whalen, Wallace 160
Whalen, Wallace 173
Whalen, William 201
White, Abraham 128
White, Samuel 270
Wight, Roy 289
Willette, John 185
Willette, William 227
Williams, George 229
Winters, Henry 176
WWI, Mourning a Fallen
Comrade 108
WWI, Soldier Captured by
Germans 101
WWII, Soldier Repairing
Vehicle, 166th Regiment,
Italy 232
WWI, Soldiers Blinded by
Gas 101
WWI, Soldiers from Strait
129
WWII, Soldiers from Stra
129

Young, Roy 240

# SOURCES

Abel, Edwin. "After Beaumont Hamel." *Arms and the Newfoundlander*, Ed. Elizabeth Russell Miller, St. John's: Harry Cuff Publications, 1994.

Andrews, Fredrick. "Beaumont Hamel." *Arms and the Newfoundlander*, Ed. Elizabeth Russell Miller, St. John's: Harry Cuff Publications, 1994.

Caulderwood, A.W. "Merchant Navy Men." Merchant Naval Association, St. John's, 1943.

MacDonald, Robert G. "Inscriptions." *Arms and the Newfoundlander*, Ed. Elizabeth Russell Miller, St. John's: Harry Cuff Publications, 1994.

MacDonald, Robert G. "Soldiers Poet." *Arms and the Newfoundlander*, Ed. Elizabeth Russell Miller, St. John's: Harry Cuff Publications, 1994.

Mars, Peter C. "Remembrance Day." *Arms and the Newfoundlander*, Ed. Elizabeth Russell Miller, St. John's: Harry Cuff Publications, 1994.

Murphy, James. "Our Returned Heroes." *Arms and the Newfoundlander*, Ed. Elizabeth Russell Miller, St. John's: Harry Cuff Publications, 1994.

Murphy, Leo. "Out of Line." *Arms and the Newfoundlander*, Ed. Elizabeth Russell Miller, St. John's: Harry Cuff Publications, 1994.

Oxenhan, John. "The Newfoundland Memorial Park, Beaumont Hamel, The Great War 1914-1918." *Military History of Newfoundland*, Ed. Jim Shields, St. John's: Naval Association of Newfoundland.

Smith, Fredrich J. Johnson. "Sons of Terra Nova." *Arms and the Newfoundlander,* Ed. Elizabeth Russell Miller, St. John's: Harry Cuff Publications, 1994.

Sparrow, E. "The Dying Soldier." *Arms and the Newfoundlander*, Ed. Elizabeth Russell Miller, St. John's: Harry Cuff Publications, 1994.

Turner, Jack. "Bill." *Arms and the Newfoundlander*, Ed. Elizabeth Russell Miller, St. John's: Harry Cuff Publications, 1994.

"Beaumont Hamel, Battle of the Somme." unpublished poem, author unknown.

"Hazely Down Camp." unpublished poem, author unknown.

"Since I Met You I'm Not Afraid." unpublished poem, author unknown.

"The July Drive, July 1, 1916, On The Somme." unpublished poem, author unknown.

"This World of Love and Hate." unpublished poem, author unknown.

"To The Newfoundlanders and the Labradorians Who Steadfast and True Answered the Call of Duty and Died in the Defence of Freedom." unpublished poem, author unknown.

All reasonable efforts have been made to acquire reprint permission for the inserts included in this publication. Where we have been unsuccessful in making contact, we have chosen to reprint the material in the belief that the author would like to have the work shared with the reading public.

# ABOUT THE AUTHOR

Francis Patey was born and raised in St. Anthony, on the tip of the Great Northern Peninsula. He is the author of five other books related to life in northern Newfoundland and Labrador. He is married to the former Agnes Bartlett of Fortune Arm, Griquet. He has one son, Christopher, living in Pouch Cove and one daughter, Joanne, living in Ontario. He has three grand-children: Madison, Melissa and Jessica.